35160X 960 SPI

35160X 960 SPI

TOGU NA

Tito Spini
and Sandro Spini

TOGU NA

The African Dogon
"House of Men, House of Words"

Electa
International

Originally published as *Togu na*
© 1976 by Electa Editrice, Milano / Tito Spini

All rights reserved.
No parts of this book may be reproduced in any
manner whatsoever without permission of
the publisher

Printed in Italy by Fantonigrafica, Venice

Design Diego Birelli

Translated by Verna Kaye-Ciappina

The fieldwork that Tito and Sandro Spini have conducted is emblematic, I believe, of a growing interest not so much in the general cultural manifestation of one of the better-known African peoples but rather in the concrete evidence of this group's creativity: the togu na. More important, in attempting to interpret the history and the symbolic motivations behind these architectural structures, to outline their evolution, and to classify them, the authors realistically face the problem of preserving a heritage that belongs to the history of Dogon agricultural communities—whether these have long been absorbed into wider economic system or still preserve their own identity and territorial independence.

The existence of communal structures in certain areas of the Dogon territory is a historical reality which today calls for enormous efforts to prevent the loss or theft of the communities' most precious works of art. This loss would also signal the disintegration of a complex relationship between man and his environment, a relationship that has been created through long struggles and, although ruled by the need to exploit natural resources, never allowed abuse.

By analyzing the architectural and decorative elements of the togu na, one can gain the most concrete evidence of the existence of a highly organized culture and also get to the heart of a unique urban planning experience from a vantage point: that of a public institution translated into architectural structures that are variable yet held together by an ethical-cultural system of unusual coherence.

Above all, the authors wished to avoid all superficial aesthetic references to the togu na as "monument"—deriving too often from the guilt generated by the ethnocentric mentality of neo-colonialism. Their commitment is best seen in their rigorous scientific approach and in their respect for a category of buildings that are an expression of the people who built them, use them, and through them achieve their own cultural and social identity.

Tito and Sandro Spini have undertaken a series of research—admirably illustrated, documented and interpreted in this book—in opposition to any rigid typological classification, and made headway towards a more thorough understanding (and protection) of the Dogon cultural patrimony. It is my hope that their study will be perceived not as a kind of "museification" of the more aesthetic elements of an exotic landscape but rather as an incentive to protect—throughout the world—all those aboriginal cultures whose identities are constantly and increasingly threatened.

Today the search for originality, for the unclassified architectural structure no longer makes sense. When entire tribes have disappeared in a few decades and other ethnic groups have been forced to emigrate, it is imperative that one take into account the link between society and environment, a link which in this book is reaffirmed, almost obstinately, in every page and in every illustration.

A symbol more of the Dogon society as a whole (in the sense of productive/reproductive entity) than of the individual, committed more to public functions than to personal interests, the togu na offers an important lesson. It is a lesson that affects us very closely, not only as scholars but also as human beings, whose responsibility is to defend and enhance those cultures that up until now have remained marginal and which must not become subordinate but rather participate as protagonists.

Enrico Guidoni

You walk toward Auteuil, you want to
go home on foot
And sleep among your fetishes from
Oceania and Guinea,
They are Christs of another shape and
creed,
Inferior Christs of darker hopes

Guillaume Apollinaire, excerpt from "Zone," *Alcools*.
Translation by William Meredith, Doubleday &
Company, Inc., New York, 1963.

New art is, above all, concentration, the
pyramid's angle shooting to a top that
turns into a cross. In the name of purity
we have distorted and then disintegrated
the object, we have penetrated its
surface. We are demanding
straightforward clarity. Art is
barricaded in its camps, with its
specialized crafts, inside its frontiers.
Foreign influences intermingle like
shreds of Renaissance's "lining" still
hanging on to the soul of our
neighbors, because my brother's soul
has dark, autumnal, sharp branches.
My other brother is naive and good, he
smiles a lot. He dwells in Africa or
in the South Sea Islands. His vision
concentrates on the human head. He
carves it out of a wood as hard as iron,
patiently, without concerning himself
with conventional relationships between
the head and the rest of the body. He

reasons this way: man stands vertical,
nature is symmetric. While working, new
relationships are formed by degrees of
necessity; thus purity is born. From
darkness we draw light—simple, rich,
luminous and innocent—different
materials, balances of form. When we
create we must respect a hierarchy of
equilibrium.
Eye—you big, round, sharp button—open
up, pierce my bones and my beliefs.
Transform my land into a prayer of joy
or despair. Cotton-wool eye, flow into
my blood. Art, in the infancy of time,
was a prayer. Wood and stone were
the truth. In man I see the moon,
the dark, the stars, metal, fish.
Cosmic elements, slide symmetrically.
Disintegrate, boil. The hand is strong,
large; the mouth contains the power of
darkness, invisible matter, virtue, fear
wisdom, creation, fire.
No one ever saw white man crumble as
clearly as I do tonight.

Tristan Tzara, *Sic*, No. 21-22, Paris, 1917.

There is no doubt that negro art has set
a great example for us. Its true
understanding of proportions and design,
its sharp sense of reality have made us
perceive, even venture, many things. But
it would be wrong to believe that because

of it our art has become mulatto. It
surely is white.

Jacques Lipchitz "Opinions sur l'art nègre," *Action*,
No. 3, Paris, 1920.

A painter cannot talk—should not talk—
about works of art, except those,
whatever they are, that inspired him.
Je te donne pour que tu me donne. (I
give to you so that you may give to me),
as the old saying goes. Which is still
valid, incidentally. Yes, indeed: only
what the artist is able to take from a
work of art in exchange for an
unconditioned admiration. Otherwise,
what's the use?
That is why negro art could give nothing
to me or to my generation. To our fathers,
its discovery had been the ultimate
shock, but we ourselves feel no more
than a sense of affection and a kind of
due reverence.

André Masson, *Chef d'oeuvre du Musée de l'homme*,
Paris, 1965.

Why did the primitives, the negroes, the
savages of Laos create such beautiful
things? Because they never saw anything
else.

Jean Cocteau, "Des beaux arts considérés comme un
assassinat," *Essai de critique indirecte*, Paris, 1932.

These are all intellectually brilliant statements, plays on words, poetic compositions, in which, whether veiled or clearly obvious, a non-democratic and even racist mentality is present, a way of explaining how much has not been seen properly, how much has not been fully understood, except through the supposed superiority of the white man and his aesthetic intelligence. But even the formal results of the African social groups should be studied within the complex relationship which springs from the link between communalism and culture.

The first African sculptures to make their clamorous appearance in the world of European culture were those seen, owned and praised by great artists (especially in France) at the beginning of this century. The first initiative to study these objects from a non-European civilization was taken by a few artists, who searched for renewal through the possession of these as fetishes to exorcise their position of dependance within the bourgeois society which held them prisoners.

The removal of these objects from their complex indigenous structures was, culturally speaking, wrong but in keeping with the climate of degradation and destruction which these cultures had been subjected to by colonialism, a violent and intrusive expression of the hegemonic class. The deterrent function of the culture caused an upsurge of interest among the middle classes, often merely a superficial fascination for the exotic concerning this unusual iconography and using the colonial power with its avant-garde missionaries to plunder the African communities of what today enriches the most important European and American museums and private collections. A few ethnological museums present their material as a thorough study of African cultures, but generally these objects are meant to be seen from a purely aesthetic point of view forming part of a European logic which is completely foreign to the majority of the African cultures themselves where myth, religion, the object and its use in the sphere of the community which produces it are indissolubly bound together.

This same African world which was subjected to these corrupting influences is now making up for this in different ways with a favorable evaluation of its own personal structures within the community, at the same time avoiding an autarchic organization.

Sekou Touré, President of the Republic of New Guinea, made a significant statement concerning this at the Negro Writers' and Artists' Second Congress: "Africa is essentially communalistic. Communal life and social solidarity give these customs a basis of humanism which could be the envy of many peoples. Furthermore it is because of these human qualities that Africans are unable to lead a life organized outside the society of the family, village or clan. The voice of the peoples of Africa has no face, no name, and no individualistic sound. However, in the places contaminated by the colonists' spirit, who has failed to notice the progress of personal selfishness? Who has not heard the defence of the theory of art for art's sake, the theory of poetry for poetry's sake, the theory of every man for himself? Whilst our anonymous artists astonish the world and whilst our dances are applauded the whole world over, our music, our songs, our sculptures are studied to reach a better understanding of their meaning, a number of our young intellectuals think that a knowledge of Prévert, Rimbaud, Picasso or Renoir is sufficient to be cultured and raise our culture, art and character to a higher level. These people only appreciate the appearance of the facts; they judge only by their complexes, their "colonist" mentality.

For them our popular songs are only valuable to the extent that they fit harmoniously into Western fashions, their social meaning is foreign to them. Our paintings? They wish they were more classical. Our masks and sculptures merely aesthetic without realizing that African art is essentially utilitarian and social....
Intellectuals or artists, scholars or researchers, their ability is valuable only if they are fundamentally involved in the thoughts, actions, and aspirations of the peoples."
Sekou Touré's words outline the new attitude which should be adopted towards Africa, that is, with understanding in analysis and collaboration in synthesis leaving the developments and changes to spring from the real needs of the people without imposing anything on their spontaneity.
In this work on a structure within the African community —the togu na— among the Dogon people of Mali, we intend to document the exponents, their closely knit structure, hoping that this may lead not to a merely formal enthusiasm but rather to a true understanding of a communalistic civilization which is undoubtedly exemplary.
The Dogon population has been the subject of wide research in the ethnographical and ethnological fields, ranging from the first research carried out by R. Arnoud in 1921 and L. Frobenius in 1922 to the complex works of M. Griaule who, beginning with the reports of the first Dakar-Djibouti mission, (1931-1932) worked unceasingly on this ground till the time of his death. Collaborators and those who carried on his work with important conclusive studies include: G. Calame-Griaule and G. Dieterlen besides members of the teams formed by him. Many other experts have carried out, and are still concluding, research at different levels and in different fields relating to anthropology, zoology, geology, psychology and archaeology. Readers wishing to go more deeply into the different aspects of a civilization as exceptional as the Dogon will find a bibliographical index for subjects at the end of the book.
In 1970, for the first time, we got in touch with the Dogon community and we were deeply moved by the magic of the place and the integrity of the relationships between man and nature, moved emotionally rather than with any desire for rational and critical analysis. It was like seeing the earth from another planet where man is not loaded down with superstructures which artificially extend his own territory. Seen from our planet the Dogon man is the crust of the earth itself and can even be said to be fused together with it. A stone, a tree, a goat, donkey, snake, crocodile or man—they are all the same size when compared with the earth. Right from the start this perfect symbiosis seems totally organic as if springing from a number of natural factors, one of which is man who has shown no desire to force or alter Nature's primordial balance. After living longer among these peoples it is clear that this balance is the result of a complex social organization which in defining its vital structure has taken the existing natural balances into fundamental consideration adapting itself to them and incorporating them into an extremely malleable network in which every being, animal or vegetable and every element finds its own proper place and function in a harmonic link which, despite the enormous natural difficulties, ensures the survival of the community.
In order to ensure the permanence of this difficult communalistic organization, in a land which is often extremely cruel, it was vital to define impassable reference points which through

cosmogony and myth could strengthen the roots of an agricultural world. The positioning of the villages; the arrangement of the dwellings, the barns and collective buildings; the natural elements; the tools and working instruments down the years and the way they are used take on ritual values and meanings which bind the individuals together in their community in an interdependent relationship with myth and religion.

Places, buildings, objects, gestures and their ensuing interpretations make up the network of this community; to get to know the component elements and the structure we thought it necessary to experience them from the inside, living in their midst.

Our cultural and professional studies, different in background and methodology from the field of ethnological research, led us to begin with the examination of the habitation as being probably the most characteristic element of the larger complex of the community. By analyzing the movements of the inhabitants of the dwelling, a diagram could be drawn up which in itself completely justified the functional arrangement of the various buildings that went to make up the dwelling of the family unit.

It was also important to ascertain that "functional" did not just mean meeting the basic needs of life but implied significant groupings from the religious and mythical point of view without breaking up the physical cellular homogeneity.

The smallest unit we analyzed, though organic in itself, is defined conclusively in the biological function in a vital relationship with other cells; this can easily be observed from the diagram showing to what extent this cell opens up towards the outside. All this presented the problem of how to extend our studies to the community, a knowledge of which depended not only on an analysis of its components but, above all, on the ergometric relations with other institutions and the first of these was the *ginna*—the great undivided family—which is often identifiable with the district.

During our research in constant contact with the inhabitants a link often emerged which was at the same time explicit and symbolic, functional and transcendental with a communal structure specifically within the district or village—the togu na—("great shelter," "house of words," "the men's house"). Whilst the *ginna* and various other institutions have been the subject of

ethnological research, the togu na (conspicuous by its size within the village and constantly mentioned to us as a reference point of fundamental importance for the community and a possible key to the interpretation of a complex secret symbolism) had never been studied systematically with the aim of assessing its multiple and complex functions in relation to all the true material aspects of Dogon life.

We expect, though within clearly defined limits, to contribute to the completion of the information on this communalistic structure; we made sketches, took photographs and collected information without any preconceived plan, and at the varying levels of knowledge of our interlocutors. The examination of this first material brought to light a number of very important points.

1) The togu na is attributed with having real symbolic power of considerable influence which even today is extremely important.

2) Stories, riddles, and mythical events are connected with the togu na forming an integral part of Dogon customs.

3) There were frequently recurring numbers with precise references inside the structures and in the decorations of the togu na.

4) The tendency of our informants to connect together into a unitary meaning both the numbers and the decorations of the togu na, when placed before the sculpture of the pillars of the frontage which is a fundamental step in coming to an understanding of the overall theme.

This unexpected picture led to our carrying out a series of evaluations in the sphere of studies carried out previously by a number of different scholars. This comparison brought to light several striking links between the information we received and the overall synthesis expressed scientifically especially by ethnologists and particularly with reference to cosmogony and myth.

We returned to carry out work in situ in 1971, 1972, 1973 and 1975, collecting as much material as possible in the form of photographs, drawings and information relating to the togu na in order to produce a classification from which to form a work plan for further ethnological research within a network of alternatives which our contribution was able to individuate.

The result of the tests and analyses carried out by us could easily have led to our concluding our research in one particular direction: that of the reading and interpretation of the signs and symbols. The informative material given is, instead, the synthesis of the taping of a considerable number of communalistic meetings which took place in the villages and especially in the togu na concerning a wide range of problems in the community.

This open empiric method allows the spontaneous formation of a vast quantity of material which corresponds to the real life of the group with its natural links with internal and external relationships, myth, religion and tradition. Many were the times we noticed that strict methodology based on concisely worked interview questions leads, especially amongst African populations, to answers influenced by the questions themselves which distort reality.

Our ideological choice, the object of our research—as a communalistic building which plays an important role in socialization—was also an important reason for using a coherent methodology in full respect and with careful consideration of a structure which became clearer and clearer to us as real life went on around us with its sorrows, its sacrifices, its hopes—all have their place in its history right up to the present.

During the exodus of the Mandé towards the area they now occupy, the Dogon camped on the banks of the Niger River, not far from Kuakoruou, the Bozo fishing village. On this occasion, for the first time, we heard of their using a special structure where they would have meetings and take decisions.

On the 25th of December, 1972, during research in the Bozo village of Sirimou, north-east of Djenné, situated on an inland marsh formed by the Bani, our escorts Tetié Contao, Amadou Komou and Bougari Komou told us this story: "When the Dogon arrived on the banks of the Niger they found the Bozo tribe decimated by famine. The Dogon camped there and built a shelter on a small plateau with eight wooden poles stuck in the ground on top of which lay straw matting; they gathered together under this shelter inviting the chief and elders of the Bozo to discuss and solve the problem of the survival of the two tribes. It was decided that the Bozo were to set off towards the lakes in the north where there was plenty of fish while the Dogon would look after the old people and children who were left behind. One day a Dogon man, realizing that a small Bozo child was dying of hunger, took him under his chief's "great shelter." Without hesitating he cut a piece of his own flesh and gave it to the young Bozo thus saving his life."

This story is well known to the Dogon and Bozo people all over their land and testifies to the blood link which since then has united the two populations. Even today the Dogon and Bozo cannot intermarry because of this "kinship." Desplanges, Arnoud and Paulme have all quoted this event in their texts but without assessing the part played by the "great shelter," a role which we particularly want to underline since it confirms that the Dogon have always used a special structure for their meetings and collective decisions: the togu na.

When a new village is being built the first building to go up in each district is the togu na. Its position is chosen by the chief, usually respecting an anthropomorphic plan, with the togu na as the head and the district as the body of a man lying down.

The togu na is therefore a basic element in the Dogon village, not just as a physical building but as an associated reference point for the whole village. The numerous functions which take place under the shelter of the togu na include: the administering of justice, the fixing of the agricultural calendar, emergency interventions (famine, epidemics, natural disasters) administrative decisions (taxes and any expenses involving the community). And moreover the togu na is a meeting place, a place for teaching and working, for rest and conversation. *Togu* means shelter (referring more precisely to the roof) *na* means "big," "great" or "mother," therefore the togu na is the "great shelter" "the mother shelter". The Dogon also refer to it as "the house of words" (words uttered in the togu na take on a value and importance which make them different from any other words), or "the men's house" (the togu na is reserved for the men, women being absolutely excluded). The togu na is usually rectangular in shape with the main axis going from north to south. The main vertical supporting structure is composed of pillars, *togu kubo*, the material used for them varies depending on what is available in a particular place. Wooden beams, *laru*, (fruit trees must never be used for this purpose) resting on the main pillars form the main horizontal structure, and branches, *sabu*, perpendicular to them form the horizontal structure on top of which lies the roof, *togu*, made of alternate layers of millet stalks, *keru* (which can grow to a length of 6 meters), to keep off the sun. The floor depends on the ground it is built on, on the different materials available and on the main function attributed to the togu na in that particular village: (mimetic look-out post, visual and metaphysical landmark or meeting place.)

The varieties in shape, size and materials used for the floor covering and for the vertical bearing structure generally correspond to the variations in the three areas into which the land can be divided geologically: highland area, rocky belt, plain.

In the highland area two very different types a togu na can be seen. In the older and more isolated villages, where the togu na serves as a mimetic look-out post, it is built among boulders; a fairly flat rock is chosen as its base and any slight uneveness in the surface is used as seating or working surfaces. As rocks like these are obviously irregularly shaped, it is unusual to find a rectangular togu na, but the main axis of the polygon is usually north-south and the length of the axes is rarely more than 6 meters by 4. The pillars, in the shape of truncated cones, with a diameter at the base of about 50 centimeters forming the bearing structure, are built with stones one on top of the other; their height ranger from 1.30 to 1.50 meters. The stones used come from erosion of the surrounding rocks in ferruginous

14

sandstone with quartz pebbels. In other villages in the highland area along the tracks, the togu na stands on a large open space at the mercy of winds and rain so that a perimetral wall on three sides is necessary instead of the pillars. The wall (between 25 and 40 centimeters thick) is made of *banco* obtained by mixing earth, *pou*—which is first dried in the sun in truncated cone-shaped blocks—with water and millet straw, *yu gudu*, or "fonio" straw, *ponserou*, letting the mixture decay until it becomes a mud which can be easily molded with the hands. The straw acts as a binding material and is used because it is a poor conductor of heat. This kind of walling is extremely fragile and its upkeep involves frequent reinforcing with plaster. On the fourth side, which is open, and in the inner trusses the structure is made of slender forked columns in wood supporting the beams which are also made of wood. Small windows are cut in the *banco* walling. Their direction depends on the prevailing winds, and they are used both for ventilation purposes and to observe anyone approaching the togu na. The floor is a rectangular platform of pressed sand about 15 centimeters high which insulates the togu na protecting it in the rainy season .The togu na in the rocky

belt is built with the further purpose of being a precise reference point or landmark among the confusion of rocks and boulders. Jutting rocky ledges are always used and are often uneven. It is difficult to find huge flat boulders; for this reason the togu na in the area are smaller (5x4 meters) and their layout has to be adapted to the irregular perimeter of the base and therefore they vary considerably in shape. The bearing structures also differ, necessarily so, in order to overcome the difficulties of the impervious ground. On the rock platforms the pillars are in stone, *banco*, or stone covered with *banco;* they nearly always have a truncated-cone shape with the base approximately 60 centimeters wide and the height varying from 1.30 to 1.50 meters.

Into the stone structure of these togu na are inserted wooden pillars in kilé wood (*Prosopis africana*) characteristic of the togu na on the Séno plain. Occasionally the *banco* pillars are decorated with bas-reliefs, while on the wooden ones are carved signs and symbols of the cosmogony and Dogon myth. Where different rock levels must be used to advantage, the bearing structure is a mixture of pillars, continuous walling made of stones and natural walls in rock.

In the Bamba territory and in a few other villages the togu na is circular in shape and the floor is then made up of huge slabs of stone placed side by side. The bearing structure is composed of perimetric pillars, sections of walling and a central pillar. The roof, to fit in with the plan, is like an upturned truncated cone.

On the Séno plain the pillars of the togu na are made exclusively of kilé (*Prosopis africana*), a very hard wood which is the least likely of the African woods to be attacked by termites and is therefore the most durable. The average diameter of this tree is 60 centimeters but it can be as much as I meter in the most impressive specimens. The use of wood for the togu na on the plain is explained by the presence of a large forest which stretches from the foot of the rocky belt for over 15 kilometers down onto the Séno plain; in this area up to now the kilé has not succumbed to the indiscriminate deforestation being carried out by recent settlements. The trunk of this tree, when it reaches a height of 1.80 meters, bifurcates and after about 30 centimeters starts to branch; to make the pillars, the tree is cut from its base as far as the bifurcation so that this serves as a support for the horizontal structure of the roof. The pillar and bifurcation are in a single piece with the same grain running through, a factor which guarantees its resistance to the weight of the covering which is, on an average, over 20,000 kilos; furthermore the structure has grown naturally into the shape required and does not need any further work.

The trunk is sawn vertically to the thickness required both for simple pillars and for blocks on which to carry out the carvings, always in one piece. The wood (varying in weight from 40 to 60 kilos) is driven 40 to 52 centimeters into the ground, the overall height of the actual structure therefore varies between 1.60 and 1.70 meters; the usable height, between 1.40 and 1.50 meters. Spaced between the supporting pillars, which are, on an average, 2 meters apart and do not therefore offer sufficient protection from sun and rain, other pillars are placed to act as sun and windbreaks; besides these, other lower forked pillars serve as props used by the rope-makers for their work.

The pillars in these togu na are always, or were originally anyway, richly carved with symbols referring to the mythology or life of the community.

In the villages on the plain the characteristics of the land make it possible to build perfectly rectangular and larger togu na. The largest one we measured was in the village of Beniema-na, district of Tomi, with the longer sides 9.20 meters and the shorter ones 7.88 meters.

It is evident from this example, however, that the togu na is small enough to allow a word expressed calmly in a normal voice to be heard by everyone sitting under the great shelter. Huge planks, *tenu kubo*, are placed on the floor of pressed sand. They are cut from soft wood trees, generally cassia (*Cassia nigricans*), on which men's bodies have left their mark over the years.

Having analyzed the varying elements in the togu na in relation to their different positioning in the three areas populated by the Dogon, only the roof remains unchangeable as far as its material is concerned and the way it is built which suggests a ritual involving the whole community. This ritual is still celebrated today when the roof is remade, an event which takes place every ten to fifteen years, this period being the maximum duration for a fragile material like millet straw which is constantly exposed to the violence of sun, wind and rain. The decision is made by the elders and especially the chief of the togu na who is responsible for it. In the year chosen for this there must have been a good harvest of millet both for the beer, *(dolo)*, which is given out in huge quantities to all present and for the stalks used for making the fagots necessary to form the different strata of the covering.

Besides the inhabitants of that particular village, all the emigrants living elsewhere are informed and return for the occasion after the decision has been made in the togu na itself. One day in the dry season men and women attend the ritual ceremony instead of working in the fields. Every married man must carry four loads; every youth, six, each load being composed of fagots of maize stalks weighing about 12 kilos. Each of the emigrants present at the ceremony does his share with at least one fagot, children must collaborate and help the adults. Voluntary labor is also offered by the surrounding villages whose inhabitants will be present and they will not be forgotten when it comes to the time for handing out the millet beer.

Work begins with the removal of the old remaining straw which is handed to the old women; by burning it they will obtain potash to use as seasoning for foods and to mix with the tobacco they chew. The old people place the first layer of fagots slowly and carefully pressing the edges with a board; the adults and the young people place other layers on top, each one about one meter thick and with the stalks arranged in a crisscross fashion.

When the work is done they all settle down for a rest in the shade as they wait to drink their millet beer carried to the togu na in big earthen jars. The oldest man in the village pours a little of the beer on the base of one of the columns saying softly the words: "Amma (God) provide the togu with a good head. Amma give us a long life. Amma protect us from bad words, take your water and drink." (We were told, though we could not get any direct proof of this, that when the togu na is being built a ritual drawing is made on the base of a pillar, analogous to the ones on the bases of the sacrificial altars.)

A further similarity between all togu na is the reduced height inside which makes it impossible to stand upright. Why should a building intended to be used for so many important purposes within the community be so low as to force men to stay sitting down? We had several different answers to this question both right in the villages and from authoritative texts by ethnologists who have worked in these places. The greatly varying replies, which defy rational examination, bring out once again the great truth among the Dogon where levels are respected not as a hierarchy of knowledge, but bearing witness to the complexity of the world due to which there cannot be correct or incorrect answers but only answers presenting knowledge and the solution of a problem in different ways.

— Kodjo Ambaria from the village of Domnosogou told us: "In olden times the Toucouleurs and Bambara horsemen rode over the Séno plain plundering the Dogon villages and capturing their children by quickly lifting them onto their horses. The young Dogon took refuge under the togu na to escape, for the horsemen could not get in there as the building is so low."

— Kunjio Poundjougou from Oorukou: "If the pillars were higher the sun would come into the togu na more easily; being so low even the men sitting round the edges are protected from its rays."

— Amborgo Togo from Beniema-na: "The kilé tree has a short trunk which does not grow to more than 2 meters in height; it would not therefore be possible to get larger pillars."

— Arradigné Dounjou from Ireli: "You can't quarrel in the togu na; if a man gets angry he jumps up only to bang his head against the beams of the roof; he has to sit down again and he doesn't feel like quarrelling any more."

— G. Calame-Griaule in *Ethnologie et Language:* "The bodies' positions influence the spoken word or, more precisely, the latter, true to nature, is accompanied quite naturally with the positions favoring it. The 'true word' is that spoken by a man sitting down, a position which allows the balance of all the faculties, his spirit is calm, water in in his collarbone is calm, his words are both quiet and well thought out. The elders who meet for discussions in 'the house of words' always sit down; on the other hand—a significant fact—this shelter has such a low ceiling that it would be impossible to do otherwise. The man who wants to be listened to, the man who has something important to say, stays sitting down while, on the other hand, anyone sitting down jumps up if he is angry... only to bang his head; but to come to an agreement it's necessary to sit down again; you never quarrel sitting down."

Final proof of the solemnity of the spoken word uttered by a man sitting down in an African world which is not restricted only to the Dogon comes from D. Zahan in *La dialectique du verbe chez les Bambara:* "As a rule all the solemn words concerning decisions which are to be made are spoken from a sitting position. The same position is always used when important orders are issued. In fact this position endows the word with weight and stability. Any word spoken standing up is considered ineffectual and superficial."

The reality of the togu na building represents the sum of the different physical and metaphysical diagrams implicit in these answers; so in the togu na you can only sit down, you are prevailed upon to speak calmly and meditatively, you are protected from the sun, wind and rain during the heavy tropical heat at any hour of the day the great shelter is cool and well ventilated.

The different materials available in the different areas, the considerable variations in the environment and external influences (often very important) have produced considerable modifications not only in the type of togu na but in the close relationship of the building with the outside as well. The main differences correspond largely to the three areas of the Dogon land; the highland area, the rocky belt, and the plain.

The highland area, *toro*, is a stretch of ferruginous sandstone at 1500 feet above sea level; it is particularly arid and, as springs are few and far between, cultivation is difficult. For these reasons and because the land offers limited possibilities of defence against the innumerable raids by hostile tribes the highland area is thinly populated.

The first nuclei —circa 1300AD ?—were built in places where protruding rocks or isolated groups of huge boulders offered camouflage in the environment and therefore better defence.

Myth, ritual, religion and life were at that time an organic whole closely linked and interdependent; so even the togu na in these first settlements had no need to express itself by means of outside signs referring to single parts of the whole. Its bearing structure, eight stone pillars, is both deeply rooted in the myth and an essential and integral part of it.

The roof is supported by eight pillars, as judgment weighs on the eight elders who, in the togu na, incarnate the mythical eight ancestors. Furthermore, this schematic structure is perfectly adapted to the role of camouflaged look-out post played by the togu na in these villages. These factors and characteristics are widely diffused in the villages of the highland area situated away from the trails. The large trail that crosses the

Dogon highland area from north to south, from Bandjagara to Douentza, has made the spreading of foreign cultures much simpler. In the villages nearest to the trail the arrival of Islamism has upset the balance of the existing organic unity in Dogon society by threatening, modifying, disturbing some basic structures in the community. The mosque, school and political-administrative organization take on the fundamental attributes of a new centralized society, emptying and polluting the functions which used to uphold the old tribal society. This change was speeded up considerably during the French colonial domination which, in establishing its own power, evidently found enormous advantages in the presence of a monolithic society which, by means of bitter struggles and fierce impositions, had fought and absorbed the political, cultural and religious pluralism of the numerous peoples in the Sudanese territory. While basically keeping most of their structures in the society, the Dogons accepted this centralized political system, a result of the Islamic-colonialist alliance, since through colonialism, which had destroyed the resistance of the Bambara, Peul, Toucouleurs and Mossi tribes, they were allowed to settle peacefully on their lands especially in the more fertile part of the Séno plain. The togu na therefore loses its vital soul and link with the myth, keeping only a few of its functions (shelter, meeting place and place for talking and working). And moreover, as far as its physical structure and external appearance are concerned, considerable modifications can be seen in these villages due to the so called "Sudanese" architectural influences imported from Islam by the centers of cultural expansion such as Gao, Toumbouchtou, Djenné, Ké-Macina, Segou.

The rocky belt, *toro* or *koko*, is a steep rocky area with huge boulders broken off from the highland area with enormous deep caves caused by erosion. The part of the rocky belt facing south towards the Séno plain and stretching for almost 200 kilometers from Bandjagara to Douentza varies in height between 600 and 1200 feet. For over 600 years the majority of the Dogon villages were concentrated in this part since the special orographic position offered ideal camouflage and defence conditions to help in resisting the constant attacks of the hostile tribes who, both in the highland area and on the Séno plain, made it impossible for the Dogon farmers to stay there permanently. Furthermore,

the inaccessible dwellings of the Tellem and Andoumboulou, primitive inhabitants of these rocks, offered them their first indispensable shelters.
Other geological conformations through modifications in the earth's surface or erosion produced the smaller jagged rocks and rocky strips which are to be found scattered over the territory to the west of Bandjagara and north of Douentza towards Hombori. Facing the huge rocky belt not far from the village of Arnou sticking up on the Séno plain the Yougo rock can be seen as a geographical landmark as well as a religious and mythical reference point for the Dogon.
Living, or rather surviving, in this environment has produced through a communalistic effort a complex culture which finds its roots in the land and in the relationship between man and nature, in a general system in which continual rearrangements, adjustments, and modifications capable of determining the links and structures of a community are possible and necessary.
In the dry hot season from February to June with temperatures of up to 50'C in many parts of the rocky belt there is no water whatsoever, and the people sometimes have to walk all day to reach a spring. In no part of this area is

cultivation really possible, yet the Dogon manage, miraculously, to get millet, which is their staple diet, to grow on every minute strip of land among the rocks; they have found the best possible way for using the soil. Every depression, providing its boulders are not too large, is cultivated on the lines of a terraced garden closed off downhill by walls which serve to hold in place the little earth there is and to stem and keep in check the constant erosion of the rocks. Still the Dogon habitat in this rocky belt is a perfect balance between existing nature and man's wise, persevering intervention.
The extremely hard living conditions mean that a solid structure of the society itself is indispensable; it is based on a fundamental respect for the individual as an irreplaceable factor in the whole work force of the community. Man has recognized his own origin in this earth and having been sheltered and received sustenance from it, he has in turn shown diligent care for it, thus creating a symbiotic relationship with it. To enable them to face up to and bind themselves to this severe land, the Dogon have identified themselves with a myth which associates and defines supernatural events in natural phenomena creating them and

expressing them in terms of an agricultural tradition born and developed especially in the fields of the rocky belt, where it was vital to provide man, in serious difficulties, with solutions, taboos and metaphysical and transcendental hopes. The togu na is an emblematic element of this necessary and perfect communalistic organization in that it sums up all the functions which are involved in communal relationships even becoming the reference point in this countryside for the nucleus of the district in the village. In fact a flat rock which is easily identifiable even at a great distance is chosen as the site for the togu na in this rocky belt. In some of those villages the togu na stands in areas which are considered sacred because of the presence of altars, where the togu na itself is an essential part of this sacredness. Women are not allowed to enter these areas and men too must walk on a well-defined track which they have to follow with great care whilst approaching the togu na which physically and spiritually prepares the men beforehand for the meditative and reflective behavior they are called upon to show. The togu na in the rocky belt sum up in themselves all the explicit and implicit functions deriving from the ancestral positioning of this working community.

In these villages therefore the togu na for the Dogon means seeing the togu na, means knowing the togu na, means living the togu na with all the mythical and symbolic implications included in this.

For all this intrinsic globality of meanings, rarely do the togu na on the rocky belt have sign-symbols to explain their complex message belonging to the spheres of myth, religion or social organization; but they have these in the very essence of their presence (through coded suggestions that can be understood at different levels) in a very simple structure all the meanings which are not mediatory but illuminate the Dogon man in the knowledge of how to live his own reality or truth.

The plain, *manu*, which takes the name Gondo or more correctly Séno (*séno* means "sand" in the Peul larguage) stretches from the bottom of the rocky belt as far as the Upper Volta boundary; it is presumed that this plain is an outlying depression of the ancient mountainous massif, the result of differential erosions. It is particularly fertile land, flooded during the rain season, desert-like especially in the eastern areas between Douentza and Hombori with huge dunes varying from 15 to 90 feet in height. The

Séno lies at a height of about 750 feet above sea level. The region has no rivers, and the people eke out with extreme caution the resources available from the rare permanent pools and the bored wells where the water level is kept constant at a depth of about 250 feet.

This fertile land, also the site of primitive Dogon settlements which were often abandonned because of the impossibility of effective defence, were repopulated permanently after 1920 when the Dogon surrendered to French colonialism (the last of the tribes in the upper Niger area to do so) which had already subdued the populations which had for years fought against the Dogon particularly in the plain area. Once the old villages were repopulated many others sprang up at this time thus causing widespread immigration, especially among the young people from the highland area and rocky belt; the tendency was for the newly created group living in a village to be composed of a homogeneous and compact group coming from the same village. When, on the other hand, families from different zones joined together to form a new settlement, each group settled down in its own district, which then took the name of the village they originally came from. Each district has at its head (generally respecting an anthropomorphic scheme) the togu na which here on the Séno plain stands on the main trail going through the village on a large open space where a great variety of activities take place: the preparation of the thread used by the weavers, the weaving, the making of ropes with bark from the baobab tree, the sewing of the woven bands for the traditional garments and blankets. This central site encourages meetings, relationships, exchanges with anybody who moves from one village to another or from one market to another and who must necessarily pass by the togu na; besides carrying out its functions for its own community the togu na also serves to collect and give out news and information. In order to be able to recognize the togu na's position on this flat stretch of land, on the south side of the building is a huge wild fig tree whose high branches can be seen all over the village so its exact position can be easily located.

The new villages have strong ties with the old ones from which the people emigrated, for along with the old people, roots of a strong tradition were left behind. The new communities stand on a more generous land where living conditions, though still extremely hard,

alleviate the strain on these structures which collectivism had made necessary for survival, binding the individual to the impervious, inhospitable land of the rocky belt.

As there is no longer any opposition or antagonism, the relationships with neighboring tribes lead to exchanges in all sectors, and through these real and psychological barriers have been broken down. Thus the protection and defence lines, once so necessary for tribal unity and the consequent organic structure of links between myth, religion and custom, have been altered.

Despite the new conditions emerging from these modifications which to this day struggle to overthrow a secular organization, the Dogon strongly support the defence of their ethnic unity. This social structure is completely valid since family units, districts, necessary working tools, protection from disasters and the working of the collective organization are still not really separable from the village itself.

The Dogon have no written tradition, since the cultural heritage is committed to the spoken word which is the safest way of presenting the myth in the places where the myth itself originates. There is also a series of sign-symbols which acquire and develop their meanings in

in the richness of their individual and collective relationships of the oral bequest to posterity.

The most striking element bearing witness to the desire for expression in the community and in the values of tradition is the togu na, which in the villages on the plain still keeps all its basic functions and through its extraordinary iconography takes on the importance of figurative hyperbole in an agricultural tradition. In the togu na on the plain the sign-symbols, the sculptures and the references to a coded secret, although never indulging in formal complacency, mere didactic or explicit information, provide a visual metaphor of origin, that cannot survive in its integrity and in its mysterious atemporality outside its place of origin.

In comparing the research carried out by the ethnologists from 1920 onwards and our observations during the last five years, we realized that the culture of the Dogon people is undergoing a period of important change and corruption, so much so that we believe that, in a very short time, under the pressure of new dispersive influences, the unity and consistency of this culture will end in dissolution allowing the symbolic elements of extraordinary representative realism to become the mere external phenomena of a structure without foundation.

One of the first great transformations took place at the time of the repopulation of the land on the plain; the mythical and physical places on the rocky belt produced a civilization that expressed itself in the simplest, most coherent way including in every communalistic structure and in the individual's behavior the perfect synthesis of the complex structure with regard to myth, religion and social organization. This existence was lived with awareness in the daily examination which was the only way possible to safeguard the individual and the group, with this total acceptance of the unwritten laws elaborated in a close tie between real and meta-real in a myth to which only a few wise old men have the key of interpretation. The groups who come down to live on the plain find a very different environment where the integrity of the ancestral customs does not amount to necessity and indispensable justifications.

On the other hand, the close tie with the enduring experiences of their ethnic groupings influences them to translate into visible elements the secret messages previously contained in the hermetic oral tradition and in the very essence of living, thus making up, by means of the iconography represented in the togu na, one of the few "written" documents in the Dogon civilization.

The symbols expressed in these togu na can be read at different levels, representing different elements of a real world and a metaphysical world which, however, always have direct references to the life history and mythology of the people.

The information and the interpretations given to us by the autochtonous people and our semiotic studies single out and put forward the hypothesis of an integral reading of the various elements that go to make up the togu na which takes us back, with the help of the images and signs, to the primitive organic unity expressed in a whole dissertation which is summed up in one unity, the toguna. A remote possibility but one which should not be excluded entirely is the link which joins together the different togu na in one village or district or in the whole area in a single theme of which each single togu na is a part. This hypothesis is even more convincing if we remember that in the Dogo country events are celebrated altogether with a ritual involving a number of different villages; for example, the ceremony for the *sigui* or *dama* (time of purification or the end of mourning) are celebrated with a procession of masks. The *sigui* moves forward like a huge snake in memory of the metamorphosis of the mythical old Dogon; changed into a serpent he uttered human words breaking a taboo. For this reason he was killed, and death appeared for the first time among the Dogon. By analogy the track of the mythical serpent could be read as, and likened to, the messages of the different togu na. This suggestion could lead to the start of research to be carried out with the peoples in a reconnaissance and analysis of the different levels of interpretation and research on the examination of their daily life through usual and exceptional events which together would help to get a more meaningful overall picture.

In the initial stage of the change in customs which happened with slow but continual modifications, various close ties with tradition were maintained; in the last few years however, in a quickening up of the dispersive process the enervation of the close relationships can be seen which in positive terms justified the communalistic unity.

There are various fundamental reasons for the present deterioration: the young emigrating towards Senegal, Ivory Coast and Ghana—nations which are very much in touch with European and American civilization—are influenced by the typical mechanism of capitalist consumer society, and on returning to the Dogon community they no longer fit into the structure of the society into which they were born and this causes serious conflicts. State education, which in its central planning does not take ethnic differences into account, is run as far as the organization is concerned on the lines inherited from colonialism where the unifying language is still French. Students educated in this school find themselves placed before their own identity with criteria of analysis and prospects of intervention which belong to an alien logic, despite their sincere wish to get to know and get to the bottom of the mysterious foundations of their culture.

The old people who have always been stores of knowledge nowadays refuse any communication which might serve to pass on those secrets which were once the indestructible link between myth, man and community.

The considerable foreign interference attacks and erodes this perfect cultural unity, and convinced of its aberrant corruption the old people choose to let it die. This attitude becomes a physical and violent act when in the villages they decide to mutilate and deface the sculptures in the togu na so that these objects, once in the hands of thieves and merchants outside their environment, will not become instruments of trade and therefore of corruption of their culture.

Finally the intervention of national and international elements carrying out experiments on new agricultural and breeding methods on the land which, despite the likelihood of more favorable results, contributes in overthrowing the relationships between men, earth and nature, destroying the balance which for centuries has represented the basis of security for the Dogon.

All these elements contribute gradually but on a large scale even to the modification of the morphology of the Dogon village. Modern silage methods will make the barn buildings unnecessary yet they are a visible urbanistic feature of the village. As a result, even the structure binding the *ginna* (big family) in a functional and mythical diagram, the men and women's movements towards the life points, barn—house—animal enclosure, will crumble leading to the prediction that is unknown today but which could well come and which is a further deterrent in the destruction of the actual unity.

The social-political choices that the Mali national collectivity is making on a necessarily larger scale will inevitably remove the centers of decision of the actual Dogon unity, *ginna*—district— village, unifying other more functional territorial dimensions to the requirements of trade, taking away therefore the real power from the nuclei where up to the present, decisions of tribal unity were traditionally made. The togu na which has represented even in a physical sense the application point of the sum total of this strength, is destined to lose, along with its own function, all organic links with the village community.

In the larger towns— Bandjagara, Bancas, Douentza— where changes in the structure of society have logically been speeded up, the degrading of the togu na is already evident. Their presence next to the new buildings (storehouses, civil courts of justice, administrative and military offices) has become archaic. Their final destiny is even to be deprived of their sculptures which in Europe and America die like dumb, incommunicable objects whose aesthetic and commercial values seem almost blasphemous in the light of their sacred origin.

Tito Spini

The Dogon population's territory lies in the Republic of Mali, in the administrative zones of Bandjagara and Douentza, situated to the south of the Niger creek. It is, roughly speaking, a homogeneous nucleus of about 220,000 inhabitants. There are no exact figures since there are no reliable census statistics. The territory stretches for approximately 320 kilometers from east to west and for about 150 kilometers from north to south; it is divided into three clearly defined areas: the highland, the rocky belt and the plain.

No one engaged in research has so far been able to establish exactly and with historical proof where the Dogon people came from and when they settled on the land they now occupy. They all agree on a great exodus of the already formed Dogon tribe carried out sometime between 1000 and 1300 AD from Mandé towards the Séno plain but it is impossible to establish where Mandé territory actually lay. Some place it in the area to the north of Bamako (capital of the Mali Republic) in the direction of the town of Keita; others, such as Monteil, claim that the word Mandé is composed of "ma" meaning "Lord" or "King" and "de" meaning "in" or "near" —which would not then mean territory but the separation of the Dogon tribe from a dominating king or lord. Others believe that it refers to the Mali empire called, in Soninké dialect, "Mandé."

Four tribes went to make up the Dogon people: the Arou, the Ono, the Dyon and the Domno who lived as follows: the Arou at the foot of the rocky belt, the Ono and the Domno on the plain and the Dyon in the highland area.

At the time when the Dogon arrived, the steep land of the rocky belt was inhabited by a mythical people called the Tellem, about whom very little is known, who taught them how to build their houses on the impervious boulders. The Tellem had in turn learned this art from the Andoumboulou, men of small stature who were considered the first inhabitants of the earth living in caves which could be entered only by means of ropes; they also knew magic words which had the effect of breaking stones and piling them up along the vertical walls of the rocks. These extraordinarily well-camouflaged and well-defended settlements have always provided providential shelter from the attacks and invasions the Dogon were subjected to for over six centuries by the Mossi and the Kouroumba of the Upper Volta, the Sonray from Gao around 1475, the Bambara kings of Segou and Kaarta about 1700, the Peul of Macina around 1830, the Toucouleurs in 1850 (a Paul tribe converted to Islamism) and finally in 1893 by Archinard's French army. The struggles preventing the different populations from living together on the Séno plain ended with French colonialism, and this encouraged the return of the Dogon to the more fertile land on the plain.

Our research was carried out in 75 villages on Dogon territory. We chose 47 examples of togu na in 32 villages with thorough documentation on the different kinds and the elements which go to make up their uses, the mythical references and environmental coherence. In these villages, moreover, we were helped in the collecting of specific graphic and oral material of the illustrated examples with a great deal of further information which made it possible to expand and evaluate te general concepts defining the togu na. The spelling of the names of the villages was taken from maps of French West Africa (scale 200.000) compiled and published by the Geographical Service OAF (1957). Information passed on to us by word of mouth in the villages varied considerably from the names given on the map, but since these tend to vary depending on the dialect in the different areas of Dogon territory we decided to simplify the matter by sticking to the names given on the map. The names of people and things have been written as pronounced by the people speaking to us in the different villages. For printing reasons we have eliminated tones and accents in the Dogon terms. For correct spelling though restricted to the language spoken in the Sanga (highland) area, consult G. Calame-Griaule's "Dictionnaire Dogon."

We also attempted to collect information on the origins of the place names. As usual we didn't get homogeneous answers from all the villages to enable us to get the direct meanings of etymological derivations.

We got answers of three different kinds:
a) the name of the village with direct etymology
b) the name of the village as the key word in a story
c) the name of the village linked with a story or anecdote which was often fantastic (generally indicating the reasons for choosing that particular spot for the founding of the village).

We have therefore given in brackets, next to the name of the villages or districts, the information regarding its name as told to us by the older people we questioned in the village. The discussions regarding the etymons and their meanings took place in the various togu na, and on several occasions it was days before we got any information whatsoever. The old men we questioned would wait for the next important market in the area to have further consultations with other old men whose ancestors were linked with the village and who therefore knew even more about its origins.

Dia

Saredina

De

Mori

Kassa

Douentza

Kenndie

Kinde

Ninngari

Ireban

Bamba

Kadiavere
Diankabou
Anakila

Kani-Gogouna

Yenndouma

Yougopiri
Yougo Dogorou
Yougo-Na

Sove

Anakanda

Koundiala

Nandoli

Diamini

Binedama

Ogol

Ibi

Sanga

Gogoli

Neni

Banâni

Pegué

Bombou

Ireli

Kamba-Bandié

Amani

Tireli

Madougou

Daga

Kon-Kon

Songo

Tenndiou

Pourali

Tagourou

Domnosogou
Banikani

Nangadourou
Sedourou

Bandjagara

Barapire
Bande

Niongono

Somanagoro

Koko

Sassambourou

Dourou

Bereli

Youdiou

Patin

Souan

Ouroukou

Ogodourou

Koporokenie-Pe

Tourou

Dangatene

Wol Maouhdé

Woro

Beniema-na
Beniema

Pomboro-Dodiou

Sassougo

Koporokenie-Na

Tina

Pel

Bancas

Koro

0   5   10   15 Km.

VILLAGES

MORI

In the cave of Barkomo, one of the sacred places in the animistic Dogon religion, important ritual sacrifies take place. The altar is cone-shaped and made of *banco* and the sacrifice consists of pouring a mixture of water, white millet and the blood from slaughtered animals .The altar is a phallic symbol and the entrance to the cave obviously reproduces the labia of the female sexual organ. The anthropomorphism helps to reinforce through this representation the concept of fertile unity in which the two sexes are bound together. (There are innumerable examples in Dogon customs: the cone-shaped barn—phallic—is a container for fertility and therefore female too; the stone quarry; the *karité* oil press is feminine but carries out its function when completed by the masculine pestle).

The guardian of the Barkomo cave is Kanda, a centenarian priest whose ritual companion is the mythical snake who watches over the dark recesses of the cave. There is a close mysterious link between the two, the snake washes the priest with its saliva. It is the only one allowed to approach him and to go into the secret places in the cave. Indisputable are the judgements pronounced by the priest in the cave of Barkomo on any controversy which might spring up in the surrounding villages of the area; when he places his sacred sticks on the ground performing justice, the quarrel must end immediately.

Mori, "the group" is made up of nine districts: Dammada, Nemme, Madougou, Tebeguie, Toda, Matanga, Dagada, Dimbou, Semeli—with about 3500 inhabitants. The village is expanding rapidly and the Islamic religion has a strong influence at all levels but especially on the young people; despite this, a tacit understanding allows the animists to keep their own communal structure, including the togu na which, however, is losing its original function of place where decisions were made, for it is limited in its use to being a mere meeting center and a place of rest. In the district of Dammada ("the oldest one") at the foot of the hill where the togu na stands on, divided off by stones is the field of the Hogon (a person who performs religious ceremonies); only beer made from the millet grown in this field can be used for the ritual offerings.

The Arou tribe chose the Mori zone for the first settlements and they maintain that the togu na at Dammada is one of the oldest (1300?) and it is certainly one that has not been restored or altered. The Mori population suffered many attacks by the Toucouleurs, Peul Moslem warriors probably from Senegal. To escape the enemies' raids the Dogon from Mori used to hide in the sacred cave of Barkomo whose walls, so legend has it, expanded to make room for all the inhabitants of the village. Even today there is a large flat stone inside, circular in shape, which served on those occasions to mark out the space for an emergency togu na.

1

1. Kanda the "priest" of the sacred cave of Barkomo holding the sacred stick, symbol of authority and wisdom.
2. The Barkomo cave which lies almost on the eastern boundary of Mori territory in a huge eroded area of ferruginous sandstone.

2

3. The entrance to the cave reproducing the female sexual organ.

4. Pemo, Kanda's nephew, the man who officiates at the ritual sacrifices.

5. The ancient togu na in the district of Dammada. The Hogon field of millet cannot be crossed by any stranger and is therefore marked out with rows of stones.

KENNDIE

Kenndie ("successful," for a crop, for example) is a fortified village. Its territory is on a plateau in the highland area; for defence reasons the founders of the village chose a confused welter of boulders and rocks as their site. The high position and the structure of the rocks make access difficult and offer considerable camouflage. This camouflage is further accentuated in the building technique used; the walls are made of stone and only the top part of the buildings blending in with the sky is made of *banco*. Besides this, an exceptional fact, natural shapes and forms are copied for the building of the togu na with the aim of making identification more difficult. The togu na in the Godie district is hidden away among the huge eroded rocks so that it takes on the characteristics of its environment in its outline and size. The choice of material for the flooring of the togu na is made bearing in mind the comfort of the men both when sitting and lying down. These togu na standing as

6

7

32

look-out posts are particularly exposed so that in the direction of the prevailing wind (usually the armatan) huge slabs of stone are shaped and placed on top of the pillars. Eight pillars form the bearing structure of this togu na, eight being the number representing the eight mythical ancestors who came down from the sky to earth in an ark and who are now identified with the eight oldest men of the village who discuss and make the most important decisions concerning the community in the togu na.

6. The togu na can only be reached by going through this passageway.

7. The rock forming the base which has been worn smooth by men's bodies and is a perfect surface for working and resting. The traditional game of Hawele carved out of a tree trunk.

8. The togu na is perfectly camouflaged as it copies the natural rock formation caused by erosion.

9. The vertical stone slabs act as windbreaks.

8

DE

De, means "fart." The legend tells of a hunter unsuccessfully hunting his prey who, on arriving at the place where the village now stands, sat down to rest and broke wind. It is situated in a particularly open part of the highland area exposed to very high winds during the rainy season. The land has all the characteristics of shrubby savannah with very few trees and hardly any rocky formations. In building the togu na these basic limitations are borne in mind when selecting materials and the shape of the building. The shortage of stones means that the walling must be done in *banco* and the climactic conditions mean that the pillars usually used in the highland area are replaced with a perimetral bearing structure on three sides, walling in *banco*, while the structures are completed on the fourth open side with slender wood pillars.

The openings made in the outside walls

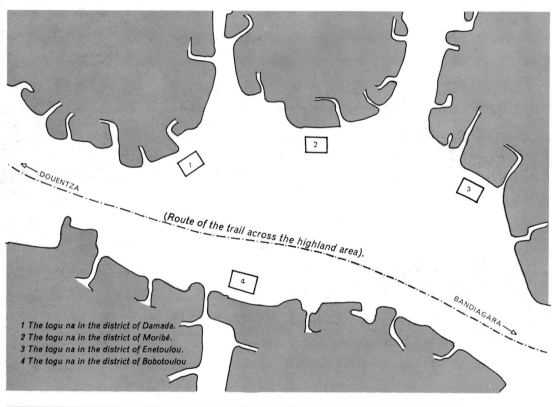

1 The togu na in the district of Damada.
2 The togu na in the district of Moribé.
3 The togu na in the district of Enetoulou.
4 The togu na in the district of Bobotoulou

DOUENTZA

(Route of the trail across the highland area).

BANDIAGARA

11

are such that they give maximum shelter while at the same time allowing somebody to look outside from a sitting position.
De is divided into four districts: Moribe ("district of the Marabù") Bobotoulou ("the slave district") Enetoulou ("the goat district") Dammada (after the district of the same name in Mori). They are arranged in a semicircle in relation to a large central area; at the top of each circular sector stands the togu na so that each building can be seen from the others, and they can all keep an eye on both the public central area and the trail connecting the whole of the Dogon highland area which passes through the village. So this position confirms the tradition whereby the togu na is the head of the district and an essential meeting point.
Besides the technical and functional reasons, the togu na in De differ from the traditional plan and are less influenced by the Dogon myth because of the strong influence which the Islamic religion has had on their customs in general and especially on their architecture.

10. The position of the different togu na in De in relation to the districts of the village.

11-13. The district of Moribe. The small openings in the walls are made as it is being built by a man sitting inside who places them according to his field of vision.

12

16

14

15

18

14-20. The Enetoulou district. Despite the Islamic influence which is particularly strong in this part of the highland area and which can be seen in the now common use of walling, the togu na still keeps some of its original functions within the community (for work and meetings).

17

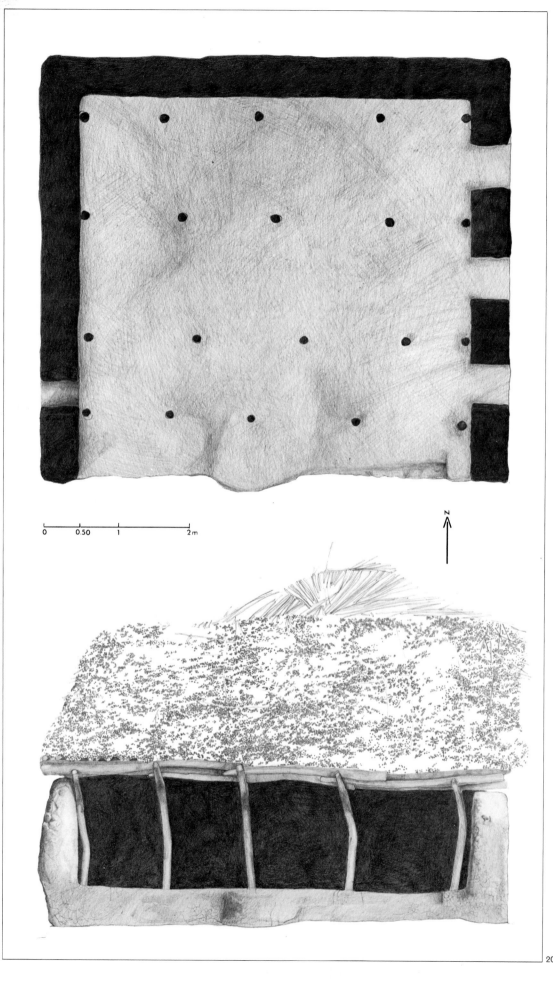

0 0.50 1 2m

N

21, 22. The Dammada district. Note the position of the togu na as the "head" of the district in keeping with the anthropomorphic design of the Dogon village.

SAREDINA

Saredina (in the Peul language "the district of the law") is a small village with about 300 inhabitants on the trail between De and Mori. Protection along the sides of the togu na, very necessary against the wind and rain, is given by the surrounding houses so that the togu na forms the center, even topographically speaking, of the community. The well located right in front of the togu na is another meeting place in the same area thus uniting the fundamental structures of the physical and social life. It should be realized that, even in areas like this where external influences have quickened up the breaking-up process of tradition, destroying the organic relationships between function-building-

mythology, the subtleties with their roots deep down in ancestral traditions are indestructible. "Well-togu na" equals "water-word"; the Dogon believe that water is an indispensable element and characteristic of wise balanced speech (the spoken word of the togu na).
As the small square becomes flooded with water during the rainy season, a supporting platform has been built with bricks and clay dried in the sun. In front of each bay of the structure, divided by the columns of the frontage, steps lead up to the togu na.

23. This village lies a long way from the main trails. In the small space the two fundamental reasons for man's meeting are joined together: drawing water and the spoken word.

23

NENI

Neni ("you got here—I brought you") like all the villages on the rocky belt, was once built into the side of the rocky plateau. The Dogon fleeing from Islamic persecution used the already existing houses which belonged to the Tellem and Andoumboulou. They could be reached only by means of thick ropes let down from above. Once there was no longer a persistent threat to their safety the villages were moved to the foot of the rocky plateau where they were still well hidden. Only the togu na can be considered a visible and characteristic element. Still today the function of the togu na at Neni is not purely as a landmark or reference point in its surroundings, nor is it only for local use but it plays an important part as a real "mother togu na." It is a place for social reuinion for all natives of Neni, even those who have emigrated to other villages. In fact in 1974 it was decided to build the school but the problem of the necessary funds was not solved until after a meeting of the elders in the togu na where it was decided to tax for this purpose every inhabitant and every native of Neni. No one dared object to the order given out by the togu na. The position of the village on this rocky belt between the highland area and the plain makes it easier to obtain different materials for building the togu na; the huge uneven horizontal slab of stone provides the supporting platform, the columns around the sides are made of *banco* while the central ones are in wood (kilé) so as to be less bulky.

On the side facing north, the corner pillar is made of *banco* and joined to the central one in wood by means of a protecting stone wall thus forming a sheltered corner for the olders. There are four pillars forming the bearing structure on the east and south sides, three on the north and west. The uneven formation of the foundation stone and spaces divided off by the columns reflect the various uses of the inside space: for meetings, rest, work and play; the game of *Hawele* or '*I*' is dug out in the stone—east-west true to tradition.

We tried to get some information while we were there concerning the significance of both the recurring numbers and the considerable inconography which appears in high relief either on the columns or carved on the wood. The great reserve and diffidence we encountered in the old people, the only ones authorized to give a reply, made it impossible to get a coherent explanation of the actual symbolism in the building. Any information given was limited to the simple definition of the immediate meanings expressed by pictures: *vilù*, *valù* and *kanaga* are three of the masks in traditional dances; the breasts, the woman, the couple and twins refer to the concept of fecundity and fertility; the footprints made by Amma's sandals (Amma is God), the sun, the lizard, are all part of the creation myth. In other villages we were given information which would enable us to venture on interpretative hypotheses of the intrinsic meanings of the togu na in Neni. However, in keeping with our decision not to embark on arbitrary deductions, we prefer merely to give documentary evidence in the form of photographs and information collected on the spot.

24. The villages perched on the rocky belt.

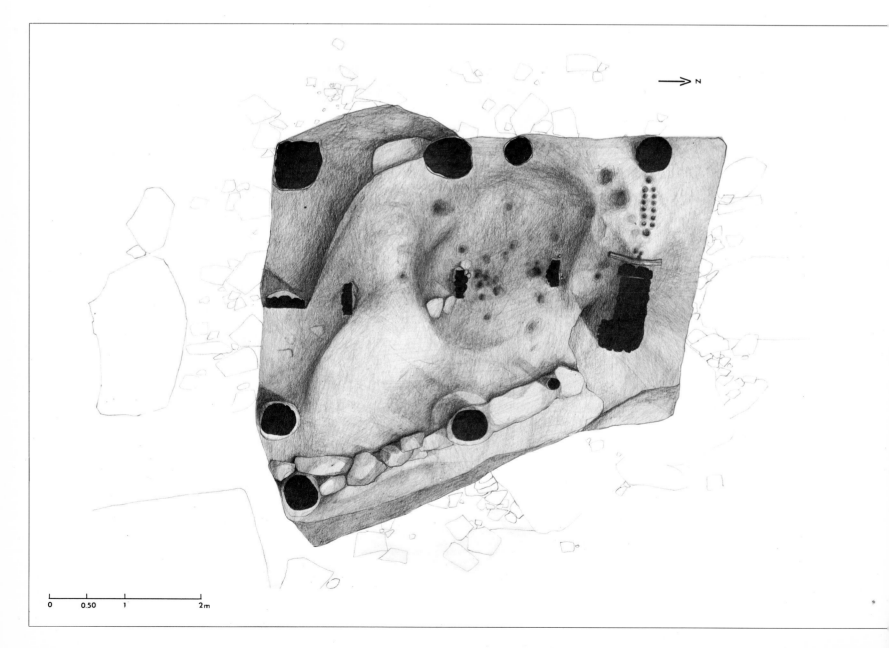

0   0.50   1   2m

N

25. Plan and drawing of east side of the togu na in Neni. The 14 small holes dug into the base are used for playing Hawele.

26, 27. The togu na stands on the one flat raised slab; it's a basic landmark in the village.

28-31. On the 4 wooden pillars forming the central axis are carved: twins (the ultimate in fertility), two female figures and on the fourth, reproduced here in the drawing, a collection of fundamental symbols. Female breasts, the prints made by Amma's sandals and the vilù mask—gazelle—evoking the role played by masks in the religious life of the Dogon. Some of the masks are in high relief on pillars made of banco and they represent the kanaga, the valù—the antelope horse.

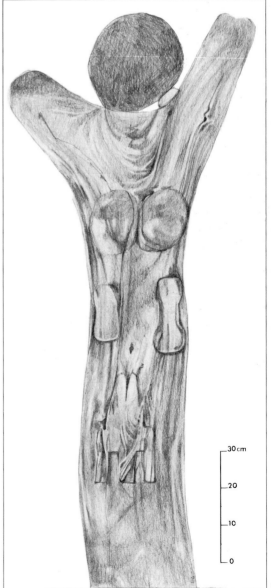

30 cm

20

10

0

28   29

32, 33. The building's uneven floor is adapted to allow the men to use it in a great variety of ways. The hollow made in the rock is filled with water to soak the fibers in for the ropes.

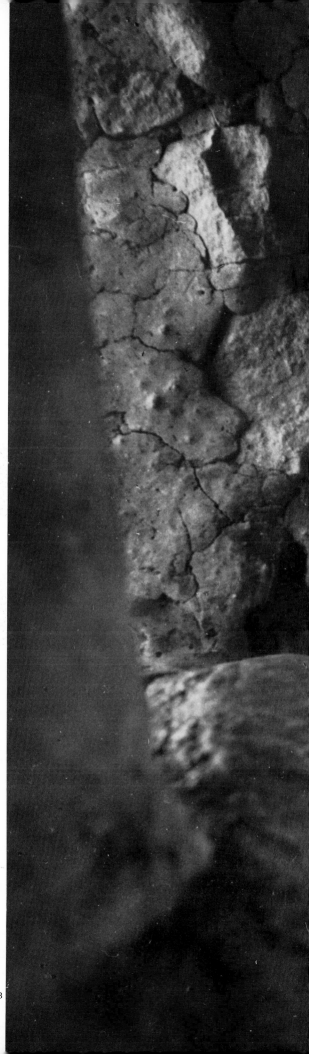

TIRELI

Tireli ("unexpected event"). The togu na in the district of Dama ("dama," "move up a little") takes advantage of the uneven ground to form three distinct levels: an underground part with a cave for the ceremony of putting on the masks for the dance in the funeral rites and the dama, end of mourning; the togu na itself, and the roof on which the men and boys sit as if from a sort of grand stand to watch the ceremonies taking place in the public square at the back of the togu na.

In the middle of this square stands a huge baobab tree whose shade for the Dogon represents "the great family." The tree is the central point for the dances and serves as a support for the huge masks on stilts. (*Tèné-táná* or *tinge-tanga*). Perhaps it is no coincidence that these masks considered by some people as being "without father or mother" are placed beside the very symbol of the great family.

34. The ceremonial dressing of the dancers in the society of masks takes place in the underground cave below the togu na (documentation by Tireli, March 1975). The kanaga mask consists of a headdress made of wood and vegetable fibers topped with a kind of "Cross of Lorraine." It is made up of wooden boards fastened with leather thongs and painted white with black squares on the joints.

35. The high rocky cliff of Daga (600ft) towering over the togu na in Ireli.

35

36. *The togu na looks out over the Séno plain.*

37. *A space for work and meetings next to the togu na.*

38. *The entrance to the underground cave of masks.*

38

AMANI

Amani ("the day of God") was a large village of about 8,000 inhabitants which was almost depopulated by the young people leaving to find work in distant Ghana and Ivory Coast. As in other Dogon villages the re-entry of these young emigrants is now taking place, uprooted from their natural environment, deluded by failure to fit into the structures of neocolonialism in Africa and sorely tried by the hard unsatisfying jobs taken.

In the togu na, besides the hypothetical ritual or the message of the recurring numbers, the supporting pillars certainly have symbolic meanings not just in the decorations but even in their actual structural shape. In the togu na at Amani the pillars round the outside remind us of the cone-shaped barns built into in the caves of the old villages; in all probability it does not aim merely at being a simple copy of the object represented but has a more complex meaning related to femininity (the Dogon consider the barn as a female container), fertility and abundance. In the togu na, used only by the men, one can always find elements of direct or indirect references to women.

The Amani totem is the crocodile; these animals which are believed to be sacred live in the pool of Koo guarded by four armed guards who spend their nights up a nearby tree to protect these crocodiles from hunters who might come from other villages. A councillor of Amani, Sirou Ato, spoke to us about this, giving information about an incident that happened in 1975. "A young man from Banani, Nio Girou, went by night armed with a gun, to the pool of Koo intending to hunt a crocodile but he was immediately caught and brought to trial at the togu na in the Ogodumo district. Atem Aninou, the head of the togu na had him whipped and tied to one of the pillars; the young man was freed only when his parents came begging forgiveness and paid a heavy fine."

39, 40. The south side of the togu na in Amani. The sirige (house several storeys high), symbol of the ginna (the great undivided family). The 8 parts of the support in this sirige remind us of the 8 Dogon ancestors.

40

41, 42. *Details of two banco pillars representing the* valù *mask and a fragment of a female figure.*
43. *West side of the togu na in the Ogodumo district.*

41

42

43

IRELI

Ireli ("The people of Sanga, having left their village, passed through Nakile and, looking down, they said—it's better here.") once a village with 10,000 inhabitants now has only about 3,000 but the village is still divided into ten districts as it was originally. Among these the most interesting is the district of Ida ("someone guilty of killing his own child on somebody else's") situated at the top of the village and, very unusual, having two togu na. One is reserved for discussions and solving the simpler problems of the community, meetings, work and rest. The other, a short distance away, on a huge flat rock, isolated and only accessible by means of a Dogon ladder (steps cut into a forked branch) is the sacred togu na. All the platform base is consecrated ground, including the altar used for sacrifices which are made on the fetish, two cones made of *banco* to the west of the togu na. Here solemn meetings are held when decisions have to be made concerning the major ritual ceremonies or if judgement has to be carried out on serious and complex questions. The hunting and agricultural calendar is decided on here with the various interventions which are of such great importance to the whole community. The two togu na, although in the same environmental conditions, differ considerably in shape and structure, and this is the result of their different functions. The sacred togu na is mainly built in

continuous stone walling to protect it from the wind and rain, a wide open space being unnecessary here as no working activities are carried out nor is a large area necessary since its use during the year is limited and the continuative period for the meetings is quite short. A further reason for the choice of an enclosed plan is to define a more reserved material and psychological space both outside and inside. The other togu na in daily use conforms to tradition with the bearing structure made up of pillars in *banco* and carved wooden poles. The central pillar on the north side is decorated with two breasts and the footprints made by two sandals (common images in the various togu na). Ama Guime Dounion, an old rope-maker, gave us his interpretation of the symbols: "The breasts represents the female who is forbidden entry into the togu na, but since man cannot live without woman, she is represented here; the sandals stand for the fact that man cannot work barefoot in the undergrowth and he therefore has to remember this before leaving the rocky ground where the opposite is true and it is only possible to work barefoot."

44. The caves on the cliff face used to be Tellem dwelling—the first inhabitants of the area—but are now used by the Dogon to house their dead. The bodies, totally shrouded except for the index finger (left uncovered to enable the body to point in accusation at the person responsible for his death) are hauled up with ropes to the openings in the rock face.

45-47. The district of Ida.

45

46

47

48

49

BANANI

Banani ("I can't go on, I'm tired") is one of the old settlements on the rocky belt and is divided up into four districts. As this village is the nearest to Sanga, there has been a recent influx of tourists since it is the most accessible of the Dogon highland places, and there has therefore been a deterioration in the ancestral traditions caused by the changes made as concessions to superficial curiosity in the folklore. A further fact that has brought about considerable alterations in the elements concerning the decorations in the togu na is the knowledge acquired by the emigrants who return to their native village after living for considerable periods of time in contact with the Baulé and the Senoufo in Ivory Coast, the Ashanti in Ghana or the Fon in Dahomey.

In 1975 renovations to three of the four togu na in Banani were completed keeping faithfullly to the ritual procedure which states that the building must be rebuilt on the same spot and must be of the same size and strucures as the previous one. All the able-bodied men living in the village and those who have emigrated to other villages, not forgetting the children, played the parts which tradition has assigned them. The main alterations are to be seen in the decorations which have become superabundant in an attempt to give the tourist a superficial account by means of the most striking images of the masks and the animals but no longer as a coded message, just simple notional lists.

In Africa in general and in the Dogon villages in particular the communal buildings and their decorations nearly always keep the anonymity of communal work. At Banani for the first time we got to know the names of the men who had carried ou the low reliefs and sculptures in the togu na. The togu na in the district of Kokoro ("found tree with good fruit, I'll settle here") is one of the renovated buildings and was completed on the 28th of February, 1975, the masks and animals in low relief on the basic walling were done by young men (the snake by Dimogo; the other animals by Abo; the *tinge-tanga* mask by Sagou

Girou; the other masks by Assegedem) in an illustrative attempt to give a generic representation of animals and ritual objects in the Dogon world. The sculptures placed around the sides of the togu na, represent according to Abinem Girou, head of the togu na: a cat, a savannah dog, an elephant, a hyena, a rabbit, a monkey, and a wild duck, all the animals that lived on Banani territory at the time when a forest covered the land as far as the rocky belt.

The togu na in the Taga district was also renovated in 1975; whilst its basic structure, copying that of the former building, correctly defines the normal use of space in the building, the cave of masks, though its shape is the same, has been betrayed in its use becoming part of a dancing display unrelated to any tradition. The breaking with tradition has contributed in to sweeping away even a sacrosanct rule about the use of the togu na. The togu na therefore becomes an instrument for commerce in that, instead of the ritual offerings of a simple welcoming ceremony of hospitality (Kola nuts and tobacco for the old men), there is an explicit request for money in return for permission to take photographs with the words "500 francs" on the columns of the togu na itself (the one in the Comunon district). Entry used to be strictly forbidden to women, whereas even female tourists are now invited to go into the togu na.

The decorations have clearly been influenced by very different styles; the low reliefs of the imperial palace in Abomey (Dahomey) for the technique; by the painted houses of Ivory Coast and Kano (Nigeria) and by the Senoufo masks for the composition and variation in color; by the elaborate and imaginative production of the Ashanti creatures (Ghana) for the drawing of the animals. The violent impact of unassimilated foreign cultures produces disruption in the Dogon tradition, despite the fact that the Banani examples represent an ingenuous attempt at an expressive renewal and enrichment of tradition.

50. The district of Kokoro, west side.
51. The district of Taga, north side.

52. Low relief in the Banani-Kokoro togu na. During the rainy season, dragged along by the force of the water, crocodiles fall over the top of the rocky cliff smashing down onto the heaps of stones in Banani.

52

53. *Layout and drawing of the west side of the togu na, Kokoro district.*

54. *The togu na in Kokoro was rebuilt in February 1975, on the same spot and with the same structural characteristics as the previous one, one of the oldest on the rocky belt.*

55. *Next to the traditional masks santinbe, kanaga, sirige are elements from the animal world introduced with expressive violence, typical of other African civilization such as Ashanti and Fon.*

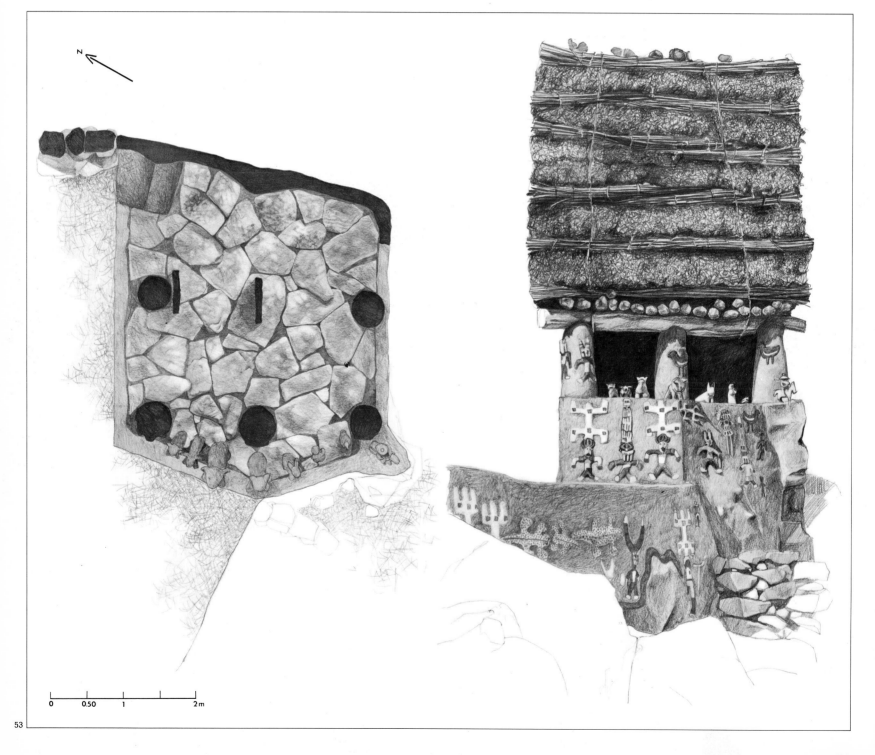

0   0.50   1   2m

53

56

56, 57. The district of Taga. Animals take over the space once reserved for the dressing of the masks.
58. Kokoro district.

57

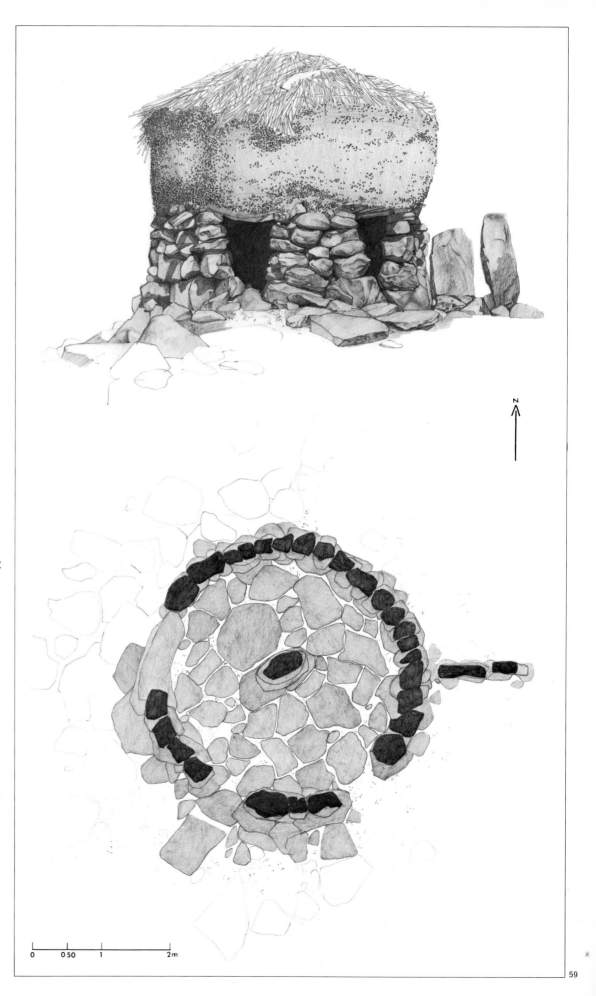

IREBAN

Ireban ("red house"—it was built with red earth) is one of the many villages at the foot of the impervious peak of Bamba, an important vantage point and landmark in the desert stretch of the trail crossing the Séno plain. The togu na in the Notaga district, like many in the area, is built to a circular plan reminiscent of the "women's house" (house for menstruating women) in memory perhaps of the time when women were also allowed into the togu na and the system was not, as it is now, patriarchal (this information came from Akoundia Guindo). It should be noted that the bearing structure consists of four elements taking us straight to the symbolism of the number 4 which, for the Dogon, refers to the two pairs of labia of the female sexual organ and therefore to woman herself.

The stone pillars are quite thick and their base is made of stones coming originally from the rocky belt; thus an environmental camouflage, which is again required for defence reasons, is achieved.

59. Drawing of the south side and plan of the togu na in the district of Dotaga.

60. In the dry season when their work in the fields is done the men do most of their jobs here (rope-making, preparing the thread for weaving, sewing the woven cloth) in the shelter of the togu na.

61, 62. On the roof of the togu na in Ireban, the pitchfork, a tool used in work and the rope-maker's symbol.

61

62

63

64. Atinbe Guindo, the head of the village of Ireban.

64

65. *Everybody is involved in community life: the boys prepare the stalks which the adults weave into baskets. The shape of these represents the world to the Dogon.*

66. *Human figures representing the family are drawn on the Pele cave in charcoal (black is thought to be purifying).*

65

66

YOUGO PIRI

Yougo Piri (or "Pilou"), Yougo Na and Yougo–Dogorou, although they are in keeping with the geological formation of the rocky belt, are, in fact, three villages situated on an island sticking up on the Séno plain.

Their isolation, and not just geographically speaking, has contributed to the conservation of the old traditions of the Dogon people; the sacredness of these places is entrusted to the safe-keeping of the old people, the only remaining inhabitants in a land where the orographical conditions will allow the survival of only a certain number of people who have made their difficult choice in the way of life, voluntarily, so as not to desert the caves, sacred altars, the togu na and the atmosphere which has always been the mythical *agora*-cum-sanctuary for important decisions and judgements which have affected the whole territory and the whole animistic Dogon race.

Yougo Piri ("one of three brothers") is a village composed of three districts whose houses and togu na are squashed and embedded between huge rocky boulders which attract and reflect the tremendous heat so there is no ventilation whatsoever. For this reason the togu na are used to the full only during the rainy season, whilst in the dry season they are abandoned in favor of the numerous caves and grottoes which serve as better protective shelters while the men are carrying out their various jobs and activities.

Caves and grottoes are dug out of the rock face about Yougo Piri; the Pelé grotto ("of the spring") guarded by the priest Barhama, is a dark labyrinth of sacrificial altars and ritual objects used for the *sigi* (a complex ceremony celebrated every 60 years—a complete cycle of human life— which symbolizes the apparition of death and the rebirth of the world). The places where other caves are is kept secret; they contain statues of their ancestors and cult objects which are untouchable in that their preservation is entrusted to supernatural events too. "Whoever enters the cave and touches these objects is cut off by total darkness and can no longer find the way out of here."

In the togu na in the Taína district, secret spaces are reserved for the making of amulets and vegetable fibers for the decoration of the masks and dance costumes.

67. *Even in extremely difficult environmental conditions (e.g. here in Taina) amongst the disorderly jumble of boulders which have fallen off the rocky cliff face, the togu na keeps its position as "head" of the district.*

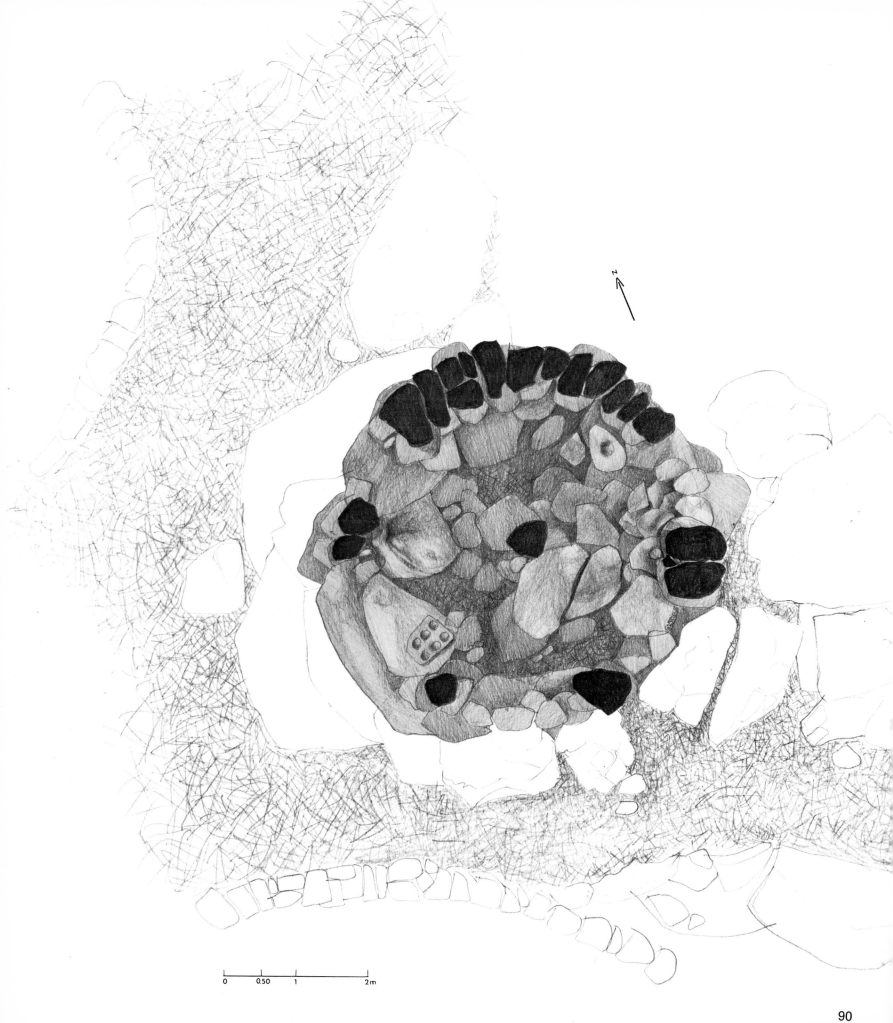

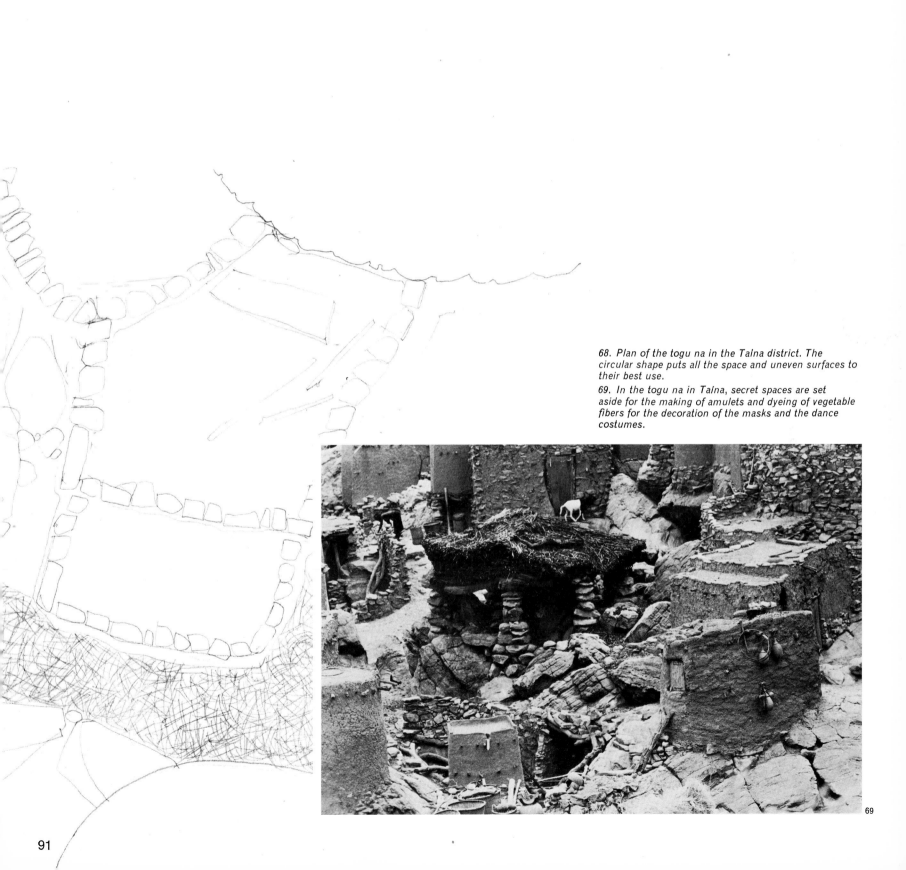

68. Plan of the togu na in the Talna district. The circular shape puts all the space and uneven surfaces to their best use.

69. In the togu na in Talna, secret spaces are set aside for the making of amulets and dyeing of vegetable fibers for the decoration of the masks and the dance costumes.

69

YOUGO DOGOROU

Yougo Dogorou ("Let's go to the bottom of the rocky belt") is believed to be the most sacred village of all. The myth claims that here the Dogon first became acquainted with death. To face up to this event, to come to a more profound understanding of it and exorcise it they created the masks, founding a society reserved for men and with secret initiation rituals which even now form part of the essential elements of the community for the religious celebrations inherent to life and death.

The mask "na," mother, the original and most important of all the masks is kept together with the fetish Albarga in the sacred cave below the highest togu na. The preeminent position overlooking the rocky belt and the Séno plain corresponds to the recognized superiority of the togu na in the Dugurey district ("sentry") over all the Dogon territory. The area, the base of the togu na where also the cave with the mother mask is to be found, is considered a sacred place. From here came the first *sigi* in their history which took on the shape of the mythical snake and reached all the other villages. For the start of the *sigi*, even when it starts in another village, they wait for the appearance of a mysterious light on the rock at Yougo Dogorou and the traditional millet beer which marks the beginning of the ceremony is offered first to an inhabitant of Yougo Dogorou, if there is one present, even if it is only a child.

All these factors mark the sacredness of the place and focus the attention and respect of the whole Dogon population on this village.

70

71. Houses and barns (up to 60ft high) among the rocks in Yougo Dogorou, a district of Tai.

71

The Dogon submit to the unquestionable judgment of the elders in the togu na at Dugurey and the fetisch Albarga with all the decisions relating to important questions which have previously been discussed but not solved in the other villages.

There are now only just over 100 people left in Yougo Dogorou, most of them playing some part in the conservation, safeguarding or celebration of the cult. A mere shadow among the shadows of his house, the existence of the great priest Agoudjou Doumbo is as if suspended. He is thought to be over 121 years old having taken part in three *sigi*—the only Dogon to have done so. Kennié Doumbé, one of the "customs officers" of the Albarga fetish, is, because of his job, completely isolated in absolute "untouchability." He himself told us that he is destined to stay in the village for the rest of his life, for only very serious reasons could call him elsewhere; then he would be allowed to take with him only a gourd full of water and may not speak to or accept food from anybody.

Yougo Dogorou is divided into three districts: Dugurey, Tai ("near the water") and Djoun ("a man was asleep in a cave, his brothers called him but he answered— go away, I shall settle here") the three togu na are set apart from the cluster of houses, sited on top of rocky boulders which make access difficult. This is to compel the men to reflect on and think seriously about the conversations to be held inside which must be free from the useless impurities man generally carries with him on normal pathways.

72. The togu na in the district of Djoun photographed from the inside of the Dugurey togu na. Both are visual and spiritual landmarks in the rocky belt.

73. The whole rock which the togu na in the district of Djoun stands on is considered a sacred place.

72

74. *Kennié Doumbo, the "customs officer" of the Albarga fetish.*

75. *The altar beside the togu na in Djoun. In the purifying sacrifices the blood from a slaughtered animal is poured over the altar as well as the millet "porridge." The choice of animal for sacrifice depends on the importance of the ritual (chickens, goats, sheep, cows, dogs).*

74

96

76. The horizontal Greek frets represent the even
regularity of the calm word as spoken in the togu na.

DIANKABOU

Diankabou (a few people in a group from
Bamba went beyond the dunes and said
"we agreed to separate") is the last village
on the Séno plain towards Douentza, an
important place for meetings and exchanges
between the Dogon and the Peul (a pastoral
nomadic people). As the togu na does not
have to be a typical reference point or
landmark like in the villages in the highland
area or on the rocky belt, and since there
are no problems of its position on the land
the togu na on the plain tend to conform
more to the mythical plan which states that
the village should stretch from north to
south like the body of a man stretched out
on the ground with his head represented by
the togu na.

The togu na at Diankabou stands on the
axis of the trail leading to the bottom of
the Bamba peak and is actually the most
northerly building whilst, as far as its
layout is concerned, it is an exception to
the rule since the main frontages face
east-west. On several pillars along the
east side is carved a slanting cross with its
topmost point on the right pointing to the
north.

The theme of femininity and fertility is taken
up on the pillars and by the symbolic number
of the pillars themselves—seven on the sides
(four meaning a woman; three, a man and
seven, the number of the couple joined
together for procreation.) There is an evident
link between procreation and the togu na
("house of words") in the fact that for the
Dogon people, words are the indispensable
element to ensure fertility in sexual
intercourse.

77

78. The togu na is also used for teaching purposes where the spoken word is the seed of knowledge for each type of manual work and for numerous spiritual initiations too.

79, 80. The male sexual organ and the upper part of the female body are represented by one symbol which comes to mean fertile union.

81. In this togu na the concept of twins meaning fertility, besides being expressed by a single pillar with four breasts carved on it, is reinforced by the upturned slanting pillar which faces it and brings together the two pairs of breasts.

79

78

80

KADIAVERE

Kadiavere (people coming from Kondou went to settle at Yougo Piri but were driven out; they went on and founded the village "driven away by everybody, but still noble"). This togu na also represents the symbolic number 7 in the columns along the north and south sides. The sculptures have been completely destroyed, losing their significance and attractiveness purposely to discourage the all too frequent robberies by tourists and antique dealers. With regard to this it is extremely important to realize that in the Dogon language "to cut off a breast" means to rape a woman, therefore the gesture of defacing the images of women in this way means double destruction: of the commercial value of the sculpture and the emblematic integrity of the woman. To prevent the contaminating of the fertility and fecundity symbol itself through robbery and commerce, they choose to carry out this outrageous mutilation voluntarily so it becomes exorcism against the sacrilegious behavior of outsiders against the community.

82. The south side.
83. A dramatic shot of the pillars which have been purposely defaced.

83

ANAKILA

Anakila ("village built and completed") or perhaps deriving from kilé (name of the *Prosopis africana*) is one of the oldest villages on the plain, not far from the trail going from Madougou to Diankabou, standing on a dune surrounded by many trees. Omar Aliou told us that under the dune lie the remains of an even older village because over the last few years household objects and the outer walls of houses have been discovered. There is only one togu na in the village and it is built in the square and is the highest point at the spot where the two trails going north-south and east-west cross. The date of construction is not known. An old man there remembered that when he came down from Kassa in 1905 the togu na was just the same as it is today, except that one pillar on the north side is now missing. It broke a number of years after and was never replaced. There are 104 pillars—all carved—whereas there were originally 105. The sculptures, signs and repetition of the number 7 (bearing in mind that one pillar is missing along the north side) express a complete dissertation on fertility. Since the heavier load of fertility is borne by the women, the bearing structures are four, whilst the other three serve to complete the building and keep off the sun. The inside of the building is divided into three basic spaces—corresponding to the number meaning "man" and more specifically those men who use the togu na. In the central part, the nucleus of the building, two sets of eight pillars are separate from the others in reference to the eight mythical ancestors. This area is without seats and is the space where a guest is placed and where the eight oldest men sit when they meet for discussion or to give judgement.

The meaning of the signs along with the sculptures on the pillars is complicated. Since fertility comes through the joining together of the two sexes there is, in abstract, a unitary and complete representation of a woman's breasts, together with the male sexual organ (penis and testicles) but only one head as the symbol of unity in copulation. The motif of the female breasts is also repeated on its own on the inner and outer pillars, being the symbol of motherhood, fertility and survival. "The breast is second only to god » is a Dogon proverb; the idea behind it is to underline the importance of maternity, fertility and survival. The horizontal and vertical Greek frets are ideograms of the word, but it is very difficult to grasp the exact meanings. In a complete representation of fertility, which the togu na in Anakila might be considered to be, the use of the word is of considerable importance. In fact, the Dogon believe that the word itself plays a part in fertility. It is actually nutritive, the seed of social relationship and is considered an essential part of procreation.

The word follows a certain course, from the person uttering it to the listener and it can be expressed diagrammatically as horizontal or vertical lines, by short or long lines depending on the level and sense of the discussion. The vertical Greek frets to be found on the edges of the pillars, even if they don't follow the irregularity, go straight on to represent the word of truth. With regard to the horizontal signs, the interpretation differs greatly from one source of information to another. The versions are as follows: the regular and calmly spoken word—the ornamental scars and tattoos the women have on their chests and abdomens—the calm and beneficial water.

The footprints at the bottom of the pillars represent Amma's sandals, the feet of the men sitting in the togu na seen from the outside, or the feet of the human figure symbolized by the pillar.

84, 85. The problem of growing old (the average age of the Dogon is 38) caused by the hard life leads to a society which places great importance on gerontocracy; the togu na is the meeting point for the different generations.

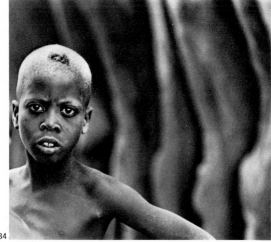

84

87

86-88. *The east side of the togu na.*

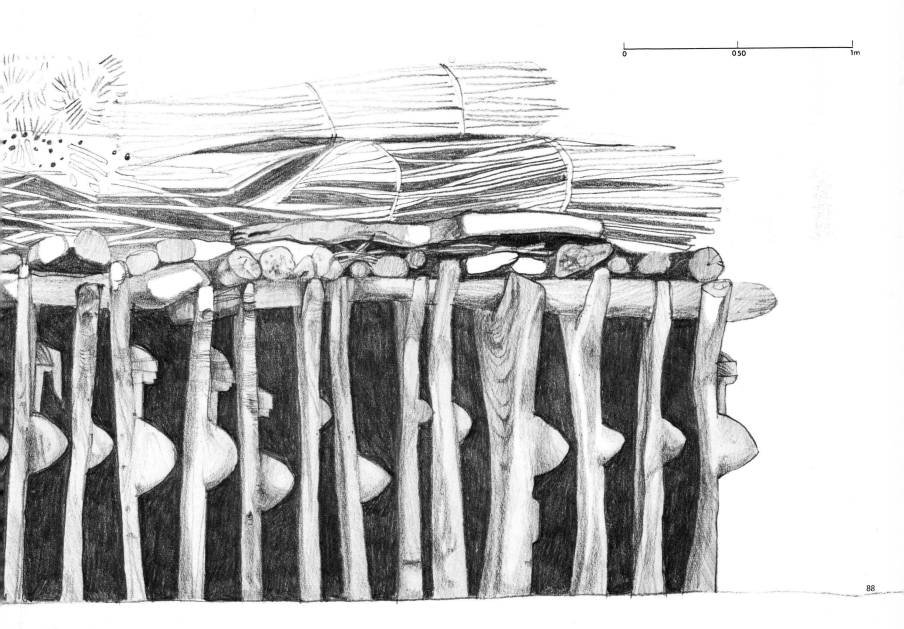

88

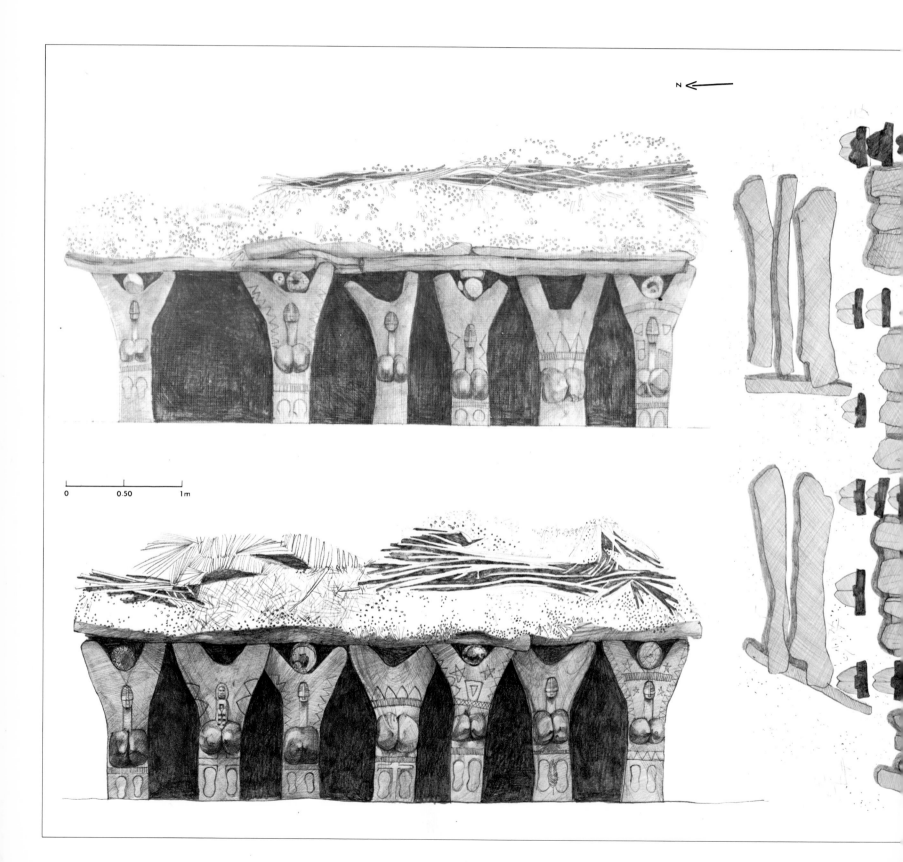

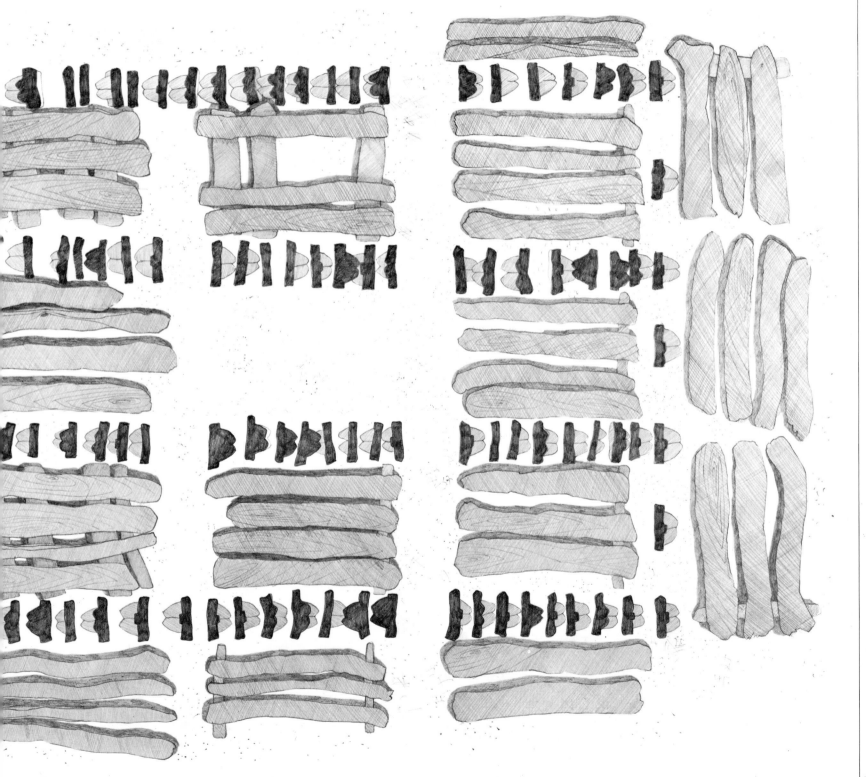

89. *Drawings of the north and south sides and layout of the togu na.*

89

90. The united man-woman symbol is repeated on many of the pillars in the Anakila togu na. It can also be interpreted as a diagram of the female body: head, neck, breasts, scarified abdomen, feet.

91-94. The first sculpture on the left on the south side represents the head of the village. To differentiate between this and other similar ones a line of brass nails has been placed on his head.

95, 96. The entrances to the togu na on the east and west sides.

97. The position of the pillars standing close together gives and extremely shady area in direct contrast with the intense heat outside.

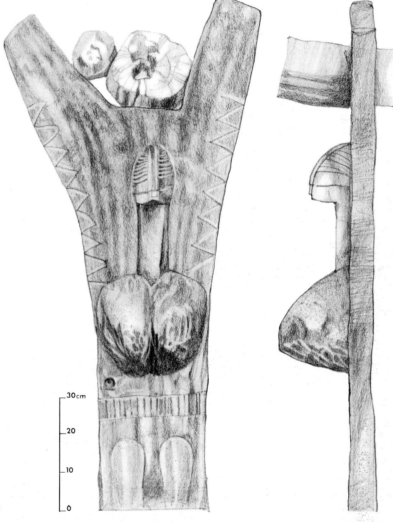

30cm

20

10

0

90

91

92

112

MADOUGOU

Madougou ("come and settle on my property"). There are three districts in the village and here too the sculptures on the pillars have been defaced to prevent them from being stolen. In the togu na in the Arnonou district (Arnonou means "people of Arou") we were told of a recent event:
— A man who had stolen a carved pillar tried to escape with it in the direction of Abidjan in Ivory Coast to sell it, but he was caught and killed after a chase lasting over a month.
This togu na is characterized by the fact that the normal arrangement of the pillars in an even line is abandoned in favor of opening up an entrance way in the center of each of the four sides marked by two pillars which face each other. The sculptures on these two pillars can almost be said to serve as sentries inspecting the people who come and go. Here woman is not represented by signs of abstract symbolism but with a grotesque, wild representation which, we were told, was the product of an ingenuous attempt to depict an Andoumboulou woman ("short people", the first inhabitants of the Dogon land: *an*—man, *doumboulou*—short.)

98. The south side of the togu na in Arnonou.
99, 100. Sculptures where the breasts have been defaced.

101

101. The carved pillars that have been stolen or
destroyed are replaced by tree trunks cut down from
what is left of the forest which once stretched as far as
the foot of the rocky belt. In an emblematic way the tree
therefore takes up its original position again.

102, 103. "To rape" in the Dogon language can be translated by the expression "to cut off the breast." 102   103

104, 105. The 2 sculptures facing each other mark the entrances on all 4 sides.

106, 107. Detail of the east entrance and the south-east corner.

105

DOMNOSOGOU

Domnosogou ("the 303 Domno villages already in existence have joined together"); the village is divided into six districts: Dogonmon, Somo, Digirou, Tobu, Ankokoro, Domno.

It is thought that on arriving at the land they now live on (1300 A.D.) the Dogon were divided into four tribes: the Dyon, the Arou, the Ono and the Domno, the latter choosing the Séno plain for their settlement. One of their descendants then founded the ancient Domno villages—legend has it there were more than 300 of them.

Domnosogou is a large village with about 7,000 inhabitants with two important trails on the Séno plain passing through it. The togu na, and especially the ones in the Dogomon and Somo districts, situated actually on these trails, are particularly important meeting points for the craftsmen who use the wide open spaces around the buildings to set out their tools for the work which is carried out in the togu na or elsewhere. The position of the togu na therefore means there is constant contact between those working outside and those working within the togu na, so that the working community is kept alive which above all guarantees the importance of the spoken word.

The interpretation of the symbols carved on the pillars is again difficult; sometimes ambiguous, sometimes contradictory. What has led to the choice of a particular subject, its position in one part of the togu na, the fact that it is placed next to the same sign or a different one, and moreover the hypothesis of a complete interpretation, are all directly linked with myth, legend, ritual and teaching.

In the togu na of the Dogomon district, the repetition of the *vilù* mask placed next to breasts, (symbol of the woman) underlines the African concept that absence draws attention to presence—that something is conspicuous by its absence. In fact woman who is excluded from the togu na is nearly always symbolically present in the sculptures. Here in particular the breasts are placed by the *vilù* (gazelle) mask on two sides of the togu na, underlining exclusion both from the togu na itself and from the society of masks.

While the togu na can be easily picked out on the rocky belt by its position dominating the village, on the plain the huge branches of the fig tree, which stick up above the barns and houses serve to mark its position. The sculptures in the togu na of the Somo district represent the exaltation of virility and place the couple at the center of interest. In fact on the central pillar along the north side a Dogon couple is depicted; the woman is on the man's left, her position even in bed, as the left side according to a widespread African belief is connected with impurity and femininity—connected elements in Dogon ideology because of the impure, ill-omened character of menstrual blood.

The togu na in the Tobu district also has this theme of the couple and fertility with the seven pillars on each side of which four have alternately carved men and women.

It is again hard to know the date when the togu na was built; we asked the old people about the one in Tobu and only got a reply after long discussions which included happenings far back in the past in an attempt to place its date; the spoken word followed its usual elliptical course involving everybody present in the responsibility for each piece of information. However the probable date of construction is between 1915 and 1918.

108. *Thread being prepared to be later woven into strips 15 cms wide and up to 40 meters long.*

109. *Drawing of the front and layout of the togu na in the district of Dogomon.*

110. *The thread being prepared for weaving.*

108

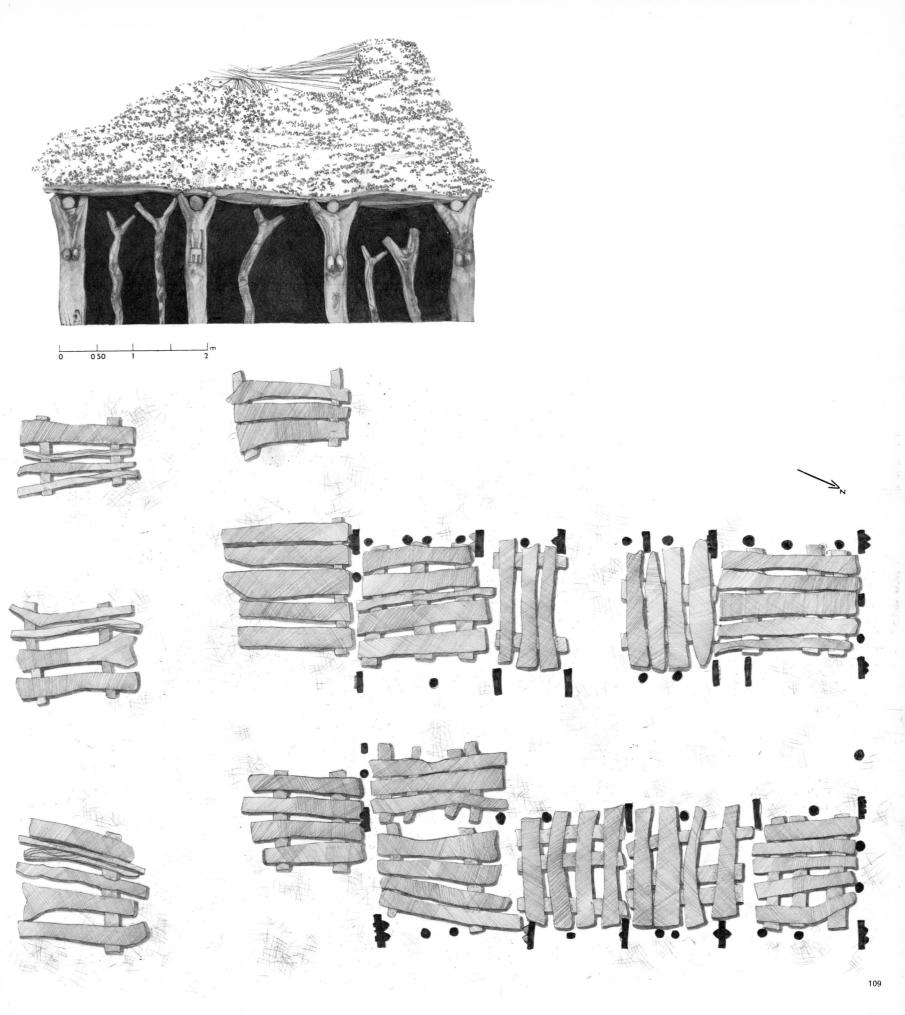

109

111-113. The south side of the togu na at Dogomon opens onto a large open space, a gathering place for the animals and a meeting place for merchants and craftsmen.

111

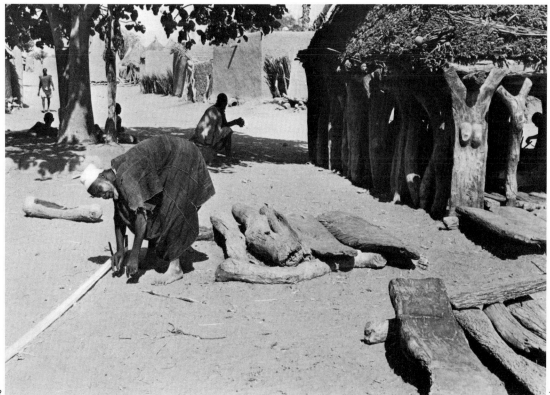

112

113

114, 115. The district of Somo. The togu na stands on the main axis of the village on the road leading east-west on the Séno plain.

116. On the pillars on the south side a figurative representation of the male and female sexual organs.

117

117, 118. On the north side of the togu na in Somo male and female figures are depicted—but not symbolically or abstractly. Also noteworthy as it is unusual is the similarity between the physical type represented in the sculptures and the actual Dogon people.

118

119. *The togu na in the district of Tobu, south side.*
120. *The togu na in the district of Tobu, east side.*

121. *The curving shape of the figure and so the effect of movement is produced as the sculptor has followed the grain of the wood to avoid having to split it.*
122. *Adiuro, the head of the Tobu district.*

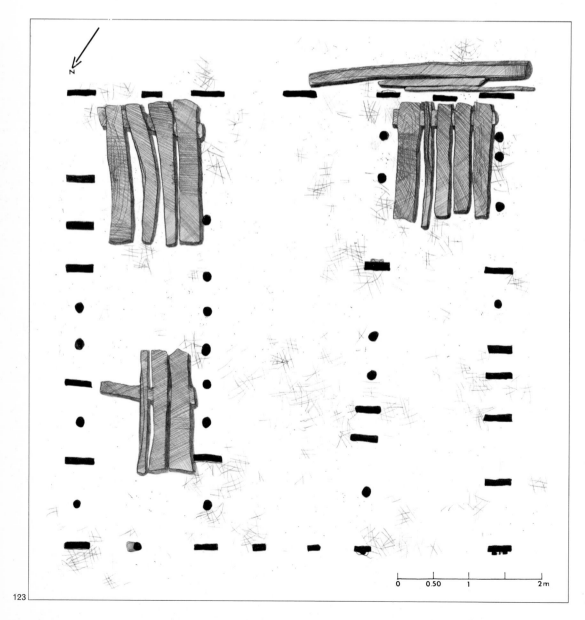

BANIKANI

Banikani ("a young couple leaves the old people and comes down to the plain to farm") is a small village divided into two districts on the trail between Barapireli (or Barapire) and Domnosogou. The district of Ibi Toubou was founded by emigrants from the village of Ibi in the rocky belt. Several of the pillars in the togu na at Ibi Toubou, which were carved over the last few years, have been substituted with others which are not decorated. So even if there was previously evidence of a unitary theory linking up the symbolism of the sculptures, this is now illegible. There are now only three sculptures left, and interpretation is necessarily limited to a single image. Here, too, we have the ambiguous hermaphrodite symbol with the double male-female meaning (male sexual organs with the upper part of the body female.) The Hermaphroditism recurs frequently in the Dogon myth: the first eight ancestors, four men and four women, were both male and female at the same time: small boys and girls before circumcision and infibulation are thought to bear characteristics of the opposite sex. With regard to the *vilù* we can find no other meaning than that of representing the dance mask of the gazelle. The stick carved into the shape of an animal is the *yò domolo* (stick of the "ritual thief"). According to the myth, the first thief in Dogon history was the blacksmith who, with a stick of this kind, stole a fragment of sun thus bringing fire to man on earth. Today in each village there are groups of "ritual thieves" composed of five men (five since each hand has five fingers and the hand is used for stealing.) At the head of these men is the patriarch who keeps the *yò domolo*; when one of the five dies the others raid the villages holding the typical stick in their left hands stealing animals (especially hens) and the owners cannot stop them as these animals are then used for the funeral ceremony of the dead *yona* ("thief").

123. Layout of the togu na in the district of Ibi Toubou.
124. The shade offered by the huge fig tree is traditionally the extension of the shade of the togu na.

0   0.50   1   2m

123

125. *The huge fig tree, which on the plain marks the position of the togu na in the village, is considered a symbolic repetition of the togu na because, they say, "the shade of the fig tree is like the shelter of the word."*

125

126. *Hermaphrodite symbol.*
127. *The* vilù *mask (gazelle).*

126

127

128

128. Yò domolo *(stick of the "ritual thief").*

129

SOMANAGORO

Somanagoro, which means "the park of horses," is one of the few villages where we were not allowed to photograph the whole togu na. Only when we went for our second visit were we allowed to take photos of a few pillars. Because of the setbacks, the information we managed to collect is very limited. The sculptures represent: the *sirige* mask (house of several storeys) Amma's footprints, the *bovidé* mask (exorcising the killing of a mythical bull), and the fox which plays an important part in the Dogon myth. We received further information about this in the village of Woro and this is discussed in the description of the village of Tagourou.

131. The Fox (vulpes pallida). According to Dogon mythology, Yourougou, the rebellious brother of Nommo, was turned into a fox.

132. The sculpture, we were told by Pendiere of Domnosogou, records the rape of Dogon women by a Toucouleur or Bambara horseman.

131

PATIN

An examination of the material collected, of the details and information concerning the togu na in Patin, in the Kounduda district ("uncle of the plain") brought to light a series of numbers with three as their denominator. The togu na was divided into three parts, and there were six pillars along the east and west sides, nine along the north and south sides.

The subjects of the sculptures (there are not many left), on first analyzing them through comparison and reference, did not give substantial evidence to enable us to link them up to the number three. At a meeting with the musician B. Calame (who has carried out some interesting research on Dogon music) while looking at a detail of a central pillar showing two breasts on top of sixty little protuberances, it came out that sixty is also the number of rhythms in Dogon music. The Dogon divide their musical notes into female high-pitched notes and male low-pitched ones. A glance at the east side of the togu na where male and female figures are alternated (or rather where there is now a pillar without any sculpture there was previously a male figure) may suggest the theory of a musical phrase. (It should be noted that the sixty protuberances are arranged in lines of six and there are also six pillars on each side.) On the internal pillars are the *vilù* and *valù* masks which have precise roles in dance rituals and particular musical rhythms related to them, as have all the other masks. Another sculpture shows a lizard, another image which links up with the masks, dancing and therefore music; it is in fact the emblematic representation of the *Kanaga* mask (one of the symbols of this in the conventional outline of the fox's body, the fox having died of thirst in the sun.) This links is even more apparent if we consider the close relationship which exists between the Fox and the society of masks; both belong to the world of the dead and of impurity, and appear in the world of the living by means of masks, dancing and music.

Yet again we tried, through talking to the inhabitants of the village, to assess whether the sculptures corresponded to the symbolic numbers we had picked out so as to obtain interpretative results which had to be in no way connected to rationalizing forces, in which case they might correspond to a European logic rather than to that of the autochthonous civilization. While as far as the direct symbolism of the single elements is concerned (despite checking of the different levels of knowledge as usual) there is only one possible interpretation of the reading: no connection emerged that could possibly join the different symbols into a unified theme.

133. A carving of female breasts and 60 abdominal scarifications (a probable link-up between femininity and music).

134. The east side in the Kounduda district.

133

135, 136. *East side. South side.*

137, 138. *Detail of the south side showing alternate male and female sculptures.*

135

136

137

139, 140. The masks are closely linked with rhythm (there is a special rhythm in the ritual dances for each one.)

141, 142. Man-woman, low note-high note; the Dogon think of the low notes as being masculine, the high ones female.

139

140

141

OUROUKOU

Ouroukou. ("We are below everybody, we are on the plain"). It is not infrequent to find in the villages on the plain the weaver who carries out his work near the togu na. At Ouroukou the weaver's loom even becomes part of the actual togu na thus forming a part of its actual structure. This symbiosis, besides being functional, has roots which go deeper into the origin of the word. The togu na, "the men's shelter," is also referred to as "the house of words," meaning a physical and social place where the spoken word is defined as taking on a precise form of usefulness, woven by experience and wisdom and reinforced by collective participation. The Dogon believe there is total analogy, which is to be found at all levels, in the relative instruments for transforming a sound into an intelligible word and thread into usable cloth. A more thorough examination of this theme has been developed by G. Calame-Griaule in *Ethnologie et Language:* "...the pegs, which hold the frame to the ground, are likened to the nerves of the skull and the front and back nerves of the jaw; the teeth resemble the comb; the tongue restlessly moving within the mouth is the shuttle; the creaking pulley, the vocal cords; the heald, the uvula moving up and down while someone speaks. The words themselves are the threads which the weaver turns into cloth...." The particular symbiosis existing at Ouroukou between the togu na and the weaving loom suggests a hypothesis for reading the numbers and symbols of the sculptures in such a way that this togu na becomes especially representative of the whole cycle from the sowing of the cotton seeds to the cloth itself and from the teaching which takes the individual from a body's whimper to a word having sense.

Kounio Poundiougo told us: "The men and women are both responsible for the cotton, except that the woman spins it while the man weaves it, the cloth is then divided between them." In teaching a child to speak the father and mother take turns conforming to specific traditional rules. The togu na is masculine with symbols of woman, the breasts and the number 4 (the number of pillars on the main frontage.) Finally the placing side by side on one column of "the men's shelter" of female breasts in a geometric pattern, which at the same time represents the teeth and the comb of the loom, synthesizes the link between man and woman in weaving and in the forming of words.

143. South side.
144. West side.

143

144

145. Drawing of the south side, and layout. On the north side you can see the shelter for loom—evidence of the close connection, even physically speaking, between the togu na and weaving.

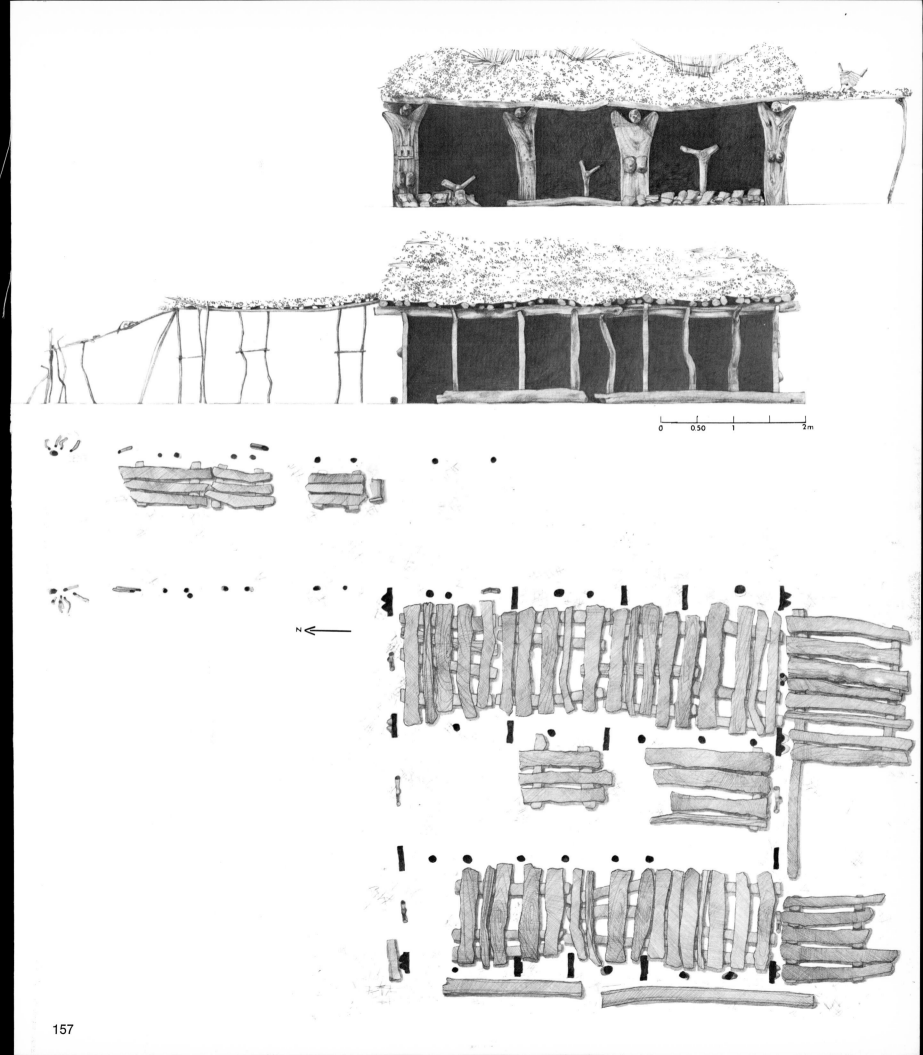

0 0.50 1 2m

N

146

146. *There are carvings of the* valù *mask (antelope) and the* dyommo *mask (hare) on the pillars along the western side.*

147. *Kounio Poundiougo, the head of the village.*

148. *The teeth above the breasts represent the comb on the loom.*

147

148

Pomboro Dodiou ("I came down first") is a village in the center of the Séno plain divided into three districts. For the togu na in the district of Tirelinoun ("coming from Tireli") a theory is put forward relating to seed-sowing and agriculture.
The representation of an antelope which in this case is a cross between a realistic sculpture of the animal and the *valù* mask, takes us to the theme of seed sowing. During the dance the *valù* mask imitates the movements of the sower digging into the ground with a stick. The sculpture of the breasts with forty small squares below it bears out the same theory. In fact, breasts are well-known as a symbol of fertility in general; the forty squares (8x5), of the work in the fields. Traditionally the Dogon field was divided into eight squares, and five stands for the number of days in their week. The number 40, being the multiple of 8 and 5, recurs frequently and as a ritual number takes on many different meanings. Eight refers to the souls of Nommo (Amma's son and symbol of order in the universe), the seeds of the collarbones, and the mythical ancestors. Five, to the cycles in the generations and to the days elapsing between

POMBORO DODIOU

149

the sacrifice and resurrection of Nommo. In this case the breasts together with the forty squares invoke fertility on the work in the fields. Again, there are a number of differing and connecting interpretations of the symbols corresponding to the effective reality and the different levels of interpretation. The same image might equally well represent simply the female breast and abdomen and scarification. The four pillars on the south side correspond in number to the Dogon agricultural calendar— the first part of the dry season (from October to January)—the dry season itself (from January to May)—the last moon before the rainy season (May)—and the rainy season (from the end of May to the end of September.)

149. *The south side in the district of Tirelinoun.*
150. *Fertility invoking a good harvest (breasts above the symbol of the field and its divisions).*
151. *Fertility symbolized by the breasts and the outline of the placenta.*
152. *Fertility in the shape of the valù mask; in dancing it imitates the movements of the farmer sowing his field.*

150

151

152

Bancas, ("a father freed his own son from prison and the latter said—I owe my freedom to my father—*ba ma kaso*, prison of the father") is a village on the main road connecting Mali and Upper Volta. It is also known as the "fish road" because trucks carry loads of smoked fish along it from the Bozo (a fishing people in the Niger joined by mythical blood relationships to the Dogon) towards Ougadougou. Contact with modern civilization detracts greatly from the functions of the traditional structures. The togu na in the

Gimboui district, standing on a large open space in front of millet storehouses is now little more than a shelter from the hot sun. Despite this the older people try to keep it in use as a meeting point for the community. Only six pillars remain of the original structure, two of which are female figures. The roof has not been renewed for a long time. The reason behind this neglect may depend on the fact that, by tradition, the renewal of the roof involves a precise ritual in which the whole community must take part including the young people who are

BANCAS

153

154

moving further and further away from their ancestral traditions and the active participation which they necessitate. Another reason is to be found in popular belief. Atem Aninou, the oldest man in the togu na at Amani Ogoduno told us about it: "When the roof of the togu na needs redoing, permission must be asked of the head of the togu na (generally the oldest man); he may refuse it while he is alive because it is believed that after the roof is completed he has only two years left to live." Therefore, as a rule, they wait for the death of the old chief before starting the collective ritual of renewing the *togu* (roof).

153. The different social and economic organizations lead to the togu na being neglected.
154-156. Bancas being nearer to the Bambara areas is affected by them even in the symbolism and representation.

155

156

157

DANGATENE

158

Dangaténé ("I am sitting here") is one of the largest of the villages on the Séno plain and one of the nearest to the border with the Upper Volta, and it has been directly influenced by the populations of the Volta which are much more Islamic than the Dogon. The result of this, as far as the togu na are concerned, is seen in the use of stout pillars made of bricks covered with *banco*, for the vertical bearing structure, and in the monumental proportions of the building which is much nearer to a village mosque than to the traditional wooden togu na of the Séno plain. Other striking factors in the unusual structure are the pillars buttressed at the base with a "shoe-like support" (in the Ireli district) which remind us of similar ones used in the mosque at Bobodioulasso.

The numerous districts of Dangaténé bear the names of villages on the rocky belt where the people originally came from. Those districts documented by us correspond to the villages of Ibi, Ireli and Neni. In the togu na at Dangaténé the pillars made of clay bricks dried in the sun are covered with *banco* and the decorations are also in this material. These are the repetition of traditional elements brought by the inhabitants from their former villages to a new culture but they only conform superficially to the noted forms without having any of the deeply felt organic reasons which converged in the rituals. The gradual disappearance of the old customs is emblematically representative of the fragility of the material used for those iconographic references which should be the means of passing on a culture. The *banco*, continually washed by the heavy rainfall, crumbles, and the images made with this material become unrecognizable, nothing like what they were originally.

157. *The togu na in the district of Neni.*

158, 159. *The district of Ibi. In the areas where the Islamic influence is particularly strong the structural and formal modifications of the togu na are evident as are also the limitations in its functions.*

159

160. The district of Ireli.
161. A detail of the typically Islamic way of fixing the structure to the ground.
162. The reading of the Koran replaces the Dogon culture of the spoken word.

163, 164. The district of Neni. In the austere Islamic architecture the triangular hole forming the window is an expression of Dogon freedom in composition.

163

164

165

166

165, 166. Banco *high reliefs on the pillars of the* togu na *in the Ireli district. They are obliterated each year by the rains but are no longer renewed as the necessary organic link with tradition is missing.*

167. Again in this togu na *the Islamic influence is clear. The long bench seat is typical of the* banco *mosques of Ivory Coast.*

167

TAGOUROU

Tagourou ("separated from Youdiou"). The fact that some pillars are missing and a number of original ones have been replaced makes it difficult to interpret the overall meaning the togu na might have had. However, several of the remaining sculptures show that the basic theme must have been a link between the creation of the Dogon world and the first mythical inhabitants. The authoritative texts by M. Griaule, G. Calame-Griaule, G. Dieterlen and D. Paulme (they are included in the bibliography and readers are referred to them for information on the subject) vary, sometimes considerably, concerning the genesis of the Dogon universe and the behavior of its first creatures. Our declared intention is not to carry out research on the complex cosmogony of the Dogon people, but to examine the sign-symbols to provide information for scholars going more deeply into the matter.

In order to help the reader in understanding the symbols we examined, which lead us through interpreting them to a synthesis of the supposed link between creation and the first creatures on the earth, we should like to give an outline of the Dogon creation myth.

Amma, the God who created all things, conceived the first human being, Yourougou, along with the Earth. He aroused Amma's anger after having an incestuous relationship with his mother, (Earth), and Amma, after having him circumcised, turned him into an animal (the Fox, "vulpes pallida")—leaving him then to die of thirst beneath the sun's burning rays. The foreskin, after the circumcision, turned into a lizard, *nay (Hemiteconyx caudicinctus)*. The Fox was then restored to life and represents even now the symbol of individual rebellion (not always in a negative sense) against pre-established order. Confirmation of this theme which

has been taken up all over the togu na might come from the 22 pillars (21 are actually there, one having been removed) which is, the Dogon believe, the number of the sun's rays and the key number of the universe.

The concept of centrality and relative symmetry is rarely found in the Dogon world; however, the togu na in Tagourou is an interesting exception since the central pillar on the north side is the one with the most sign-symbols. In fact this sculpture depicts the moon, passive witness of the Fox's incest; the sun, the instrument used by Amma to punish him, the lizard which by a metaphorical image takes us back to the punished Fox; all are essential elements in defining the Dogon concept of creation.

Also the corresponding pillar along the east side depicts, as the focal point, man surrounded by symmetry; on his left a woman, on his right the sun, moon and snake (these three all linked by impurity: death-femininity), thus accentuating the predominant role of the male in the Dogon universe. Other sculptures show the sun and moon in different positions to each other as in the natural cycle of day and night. The use of the calendar is not wide-spread among the Dogon yet in the togu na at Tagourou there is a stick hanging up with twelve notches on it (one for each month of the year); a rope serves to mark off the months and it is the chief of the togu na's job to move it. The week (composed of five days) follows the alternation of the markets. In fact the days do not have precise names but are referred to with the name of the village where the most important markets is being held on that particular day.

168, 169. The moon in different phases shows the passage of time.

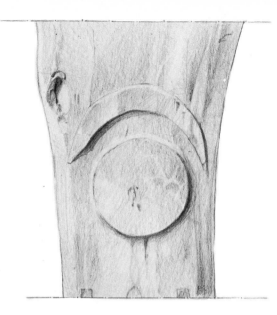

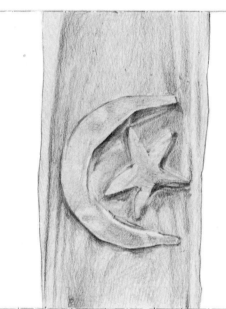

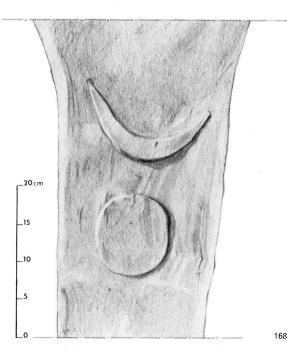

168

170. *North side.*
171. *South side.*
172. *Detail from the south side.*

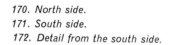

170

171

172

173, 174. The sculptures are a synthesis of one of the most important events in the Dogon creation story and the role played by the moon, sun and lizard (nay).

175. Inside the togu na the floor surface is made partly of wood and partly of sand, each part being used for different activities (work-meeting, game-rest).

174

175

NANGADOUROU

Nangadourou ("there where the oxen drink and low"). The village is divided into four districts: Ireli (where the togu na has been totally stripped of its sculptures which have been sold to dealers), Pégue 1, Pégue 2 and Ibi. In the togu na at Ibi, documented here, we met Adiourou Kodio, grandson of the founder of the village and son of Amonou, considered as one of the wisest and most respected men, for people went to him from all over the Séno plain for advice and judgement. Through a meeting with all the old people of the village present, Adiourou told us that the togu na had been built around 1930 (after the final conquest of Dogon territory by the French troops. Once the Toucouleurs, Mossi, Bambara and Peul tribes had been pacified the Dogon returned from the rocky belt down onto the plain to farm the land.) Our requests for information relating to the themes and topics dealt with in the sculptures met with no precise answer but only general affirmations concerning the fact that the topics were chosen at random and the individual choice of each sculptor depending on his personal ability. Here too, as often happened in other villages, it was obvious from the conversation going on among the old men that they did not wish on first meeting strangers to reveal the true roots of these things. The phrase used to dismiss us was symbolic of this: "If Amma helps us, as long as we live we shall 'keep' our togu na."

From the information on the different topics, from each single interpretation and an overall reading of the images and from information resulting from our conversation it can be pointed out that the togu na in the Ibi district puts forward the theory of the great undivided family, the *ginna*, through the innumerable men and women who form part of it along with the *sirige* mask (house with several storeys) the symbol of the *ginna* itself. Here too the couple is depicted with the woman on the man's left (the impure side). On another pillar the man is placed above the woman and regarding this we were told: "When a man and a woman are walking together, the woman goes first so that the man can defend her—you never know what might come up from behind." Others ironically said: "If the woman walks behind she might run off with the first man who crosses her path."

176, 177. The north and west sides in the district of Ibi.

178-181. When the subject of the sculptures is man in his daily relationships with his family and the group the Dogon represent him with direct images as realistically as possible without the use of symbolism being involved.

179

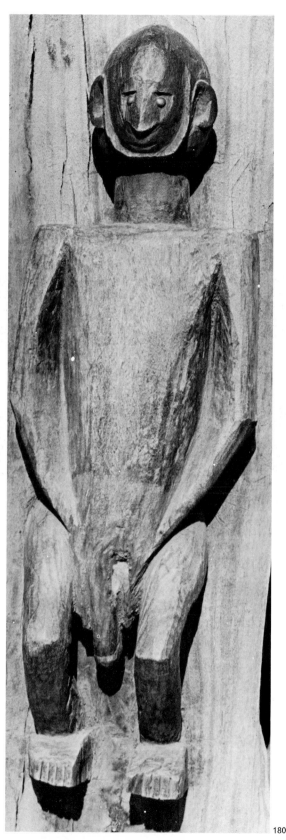

180

178

182, 183. Man and woman in two typical positions: the
man on the right, the woman on his left (the impure
side; good things come from the right, evil from the
left); the man on top and the woman underneath
(position of sexual intercourse) or the man walking
behind the woman.

184-187. In Dogon life intercourse has the sole aim of procreation. The figurative repetition and enlargement of the sexual organs exorcizes the infertile outcome of intercourse.

188, 189. Close-ups—north side.

Sedourou ("a wild cat" from "sie," a type fo wild cat unknown to us.) The togu na in the district of Ireli Canal has always attracted the interest and greed of dealers in African objects. Even in 1972, on our first visit to the place, four pillars were missing along the north side and in 1975 during our final research on the Séno plain, we noted that five more pillars from the south side had disappeared—ones that we had already examined and photographed with details of the designs. Faced with our information the old people of the togu na had to admit to having sold the sculptures. They justified themselves by saying that they had to face up to the serious problems of the community which one year of famine had caused, and these had been solved with the money thus obtained. In other villages besides this one, year by year, we were able to ascertain that important sculptures had been removed. Knowing the ease with which these objects can be sold in Europe and America, it is unfortunately very easy to predict that the togu na, bearing witness to a particular African iconography, is destined to disappear, especially on the Séno plain. Our research is now the only complete document on this important togu na in Sedourou.

The masks and the men who wear them are the main subjects of the sculptures, which leads us to believe that they are the characters in a ceremony celebrated with dances. The central pillar on the south-west side depicts the sun and moon: information we gathered tells that the heavenly bodies indicate the expiration of a period of time in events.

It is quite possible then that these sculptures relate to the *dama*. The announcement of the *dama* celebration (the end of mourning) is made a certain period of time beforehand in connection with days and moons to enable relatives and friends of the dead person who are living in far away villages to come. From the time of the announcement to the day of the ceremony a number of rules must be strictly followed: no heated discussion or quarrelling is allowed and sexual intercourse is forbidden.

The society of masks performs a determinant role in the important ceremonies for the *dama* and even today within the sphere of the Dogon community is closely linked to cosmogony, ritual and to everyday life. A complete study of this subject has been made by Marcel Griaule in *Masques Dogons*. The sculptures documented by us in the togu na at Sedourou on the remaining pillars are: the *valù* (antelope) the *kanaga* (similar to the Kommolo Tébu, a bird with red beak and feet, white wings and black head); the Fox (which died of thirst), the creator pointing to the sky with one hand and the earth with the other, the *tinge-tángá* ("the mask on stilts"), the hyena (or the hare?), three Peul women (an ironical mask underlining by exaggeration the characteristic femininity and coquetry of the Peul woman) horses and horsemen which form an integral part of every Dogon ceremony including the *dama*.

All these factors lead us to believe that the ritual dance which the togu na in Sedourou (Ireli Canal) depicts is the one connected with the *dama*.

190. The south-west side in the Ireli Canal district.
191. Drawing of the south-west side and layout of the togu na in the Ireli Canal district.

190

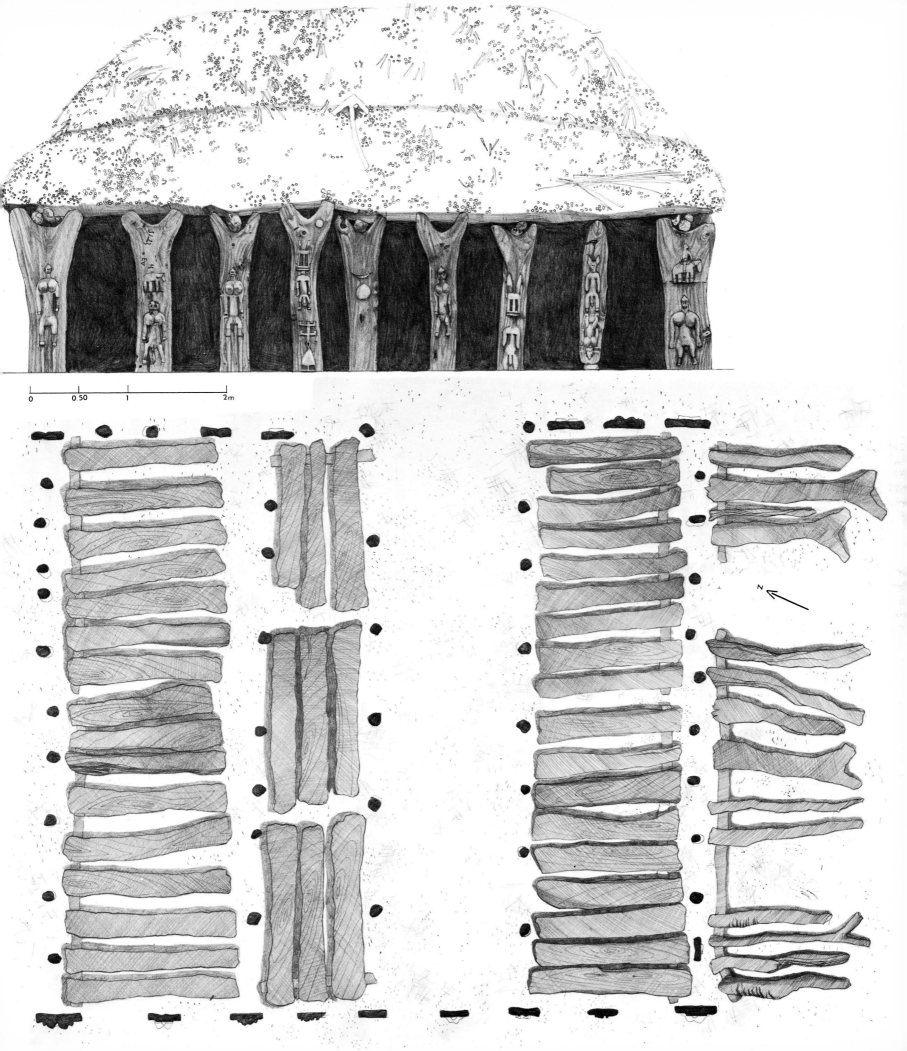

0   0.50   1   2m

194

193

195

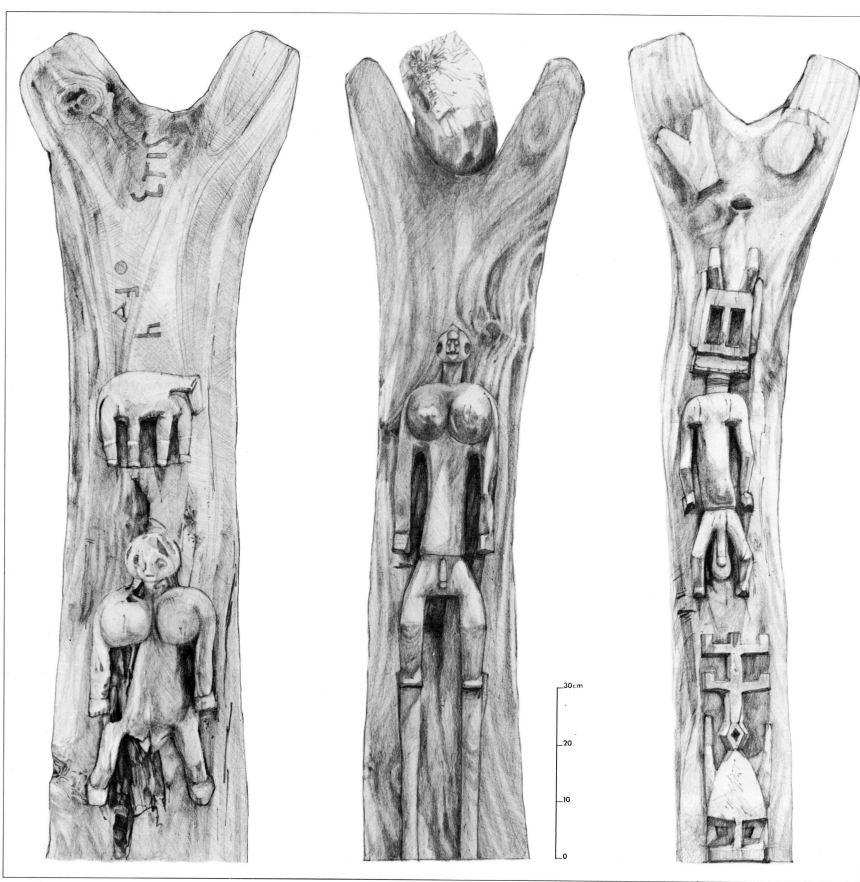

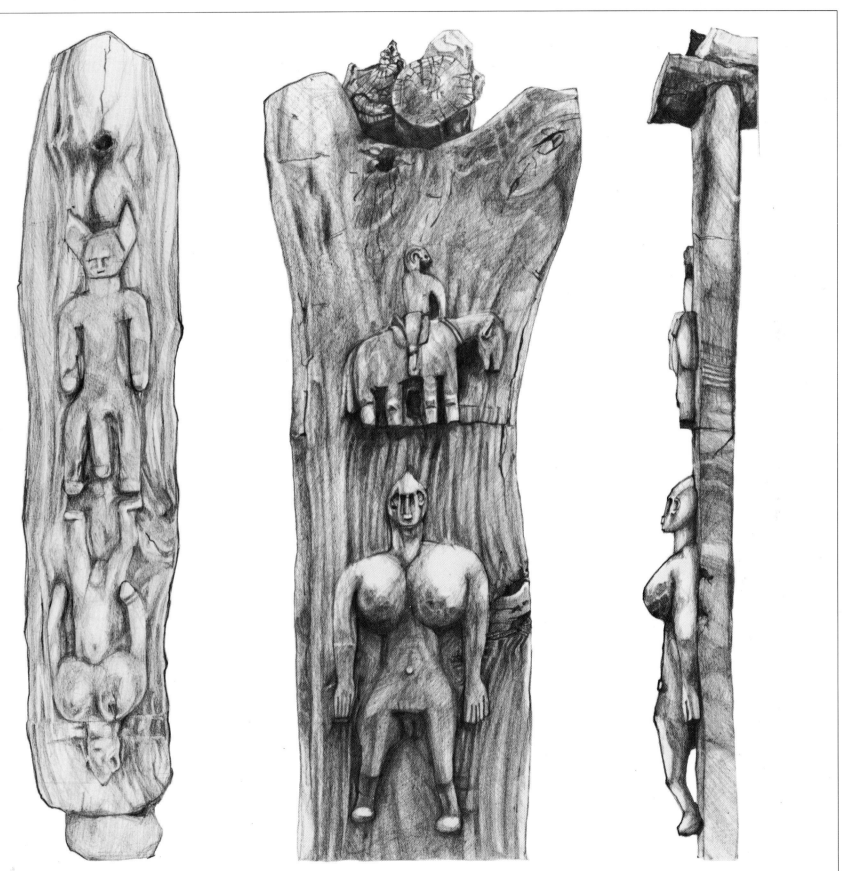

197, 198. Masks and men on horseback are significant elements in most important Dogon ceremonies. Women are not allowed to stand near the masks for fear that their impurity should prove contagious and make the women sterile or cause them to miscarry. 197

198

Youdiou (Once the *volo* berries were picked —black thorn— they sowed and reaped "a large amount of millet"). There is only one togu na in the village believed to be one of the oldest on the Séno plain along with Anakila and Woro. We got this from different sources of information and though they were unable to fix a date for the settlement they told us about the trials and tribulations undergone by the inhabitants of Youdiou. The supposed date of foundation (1400-1500?), the many times they took to flight in the direction of the rocky belt because of the raids and plundering of the hostile tribes, the return to the territory, confirm their history which must certainly have developed over a period of several hundred years. This togu na was built based on the number 7 (4+3). (Two pillars have recently been stolen from the north side and another from the west side). Each side consists of seven pillars, and inside there are seven supports dividing the areas into three parts. There are also seven layers covering the roof (four layers alternating another three in millet stalks of different thicknesses.) On the main sides, north and south, there are four supporting pillars and three of these serve to keep out the sun. It should be remembered here that four is the number connected with the woman (the four labia of the sexual organ) and three with the

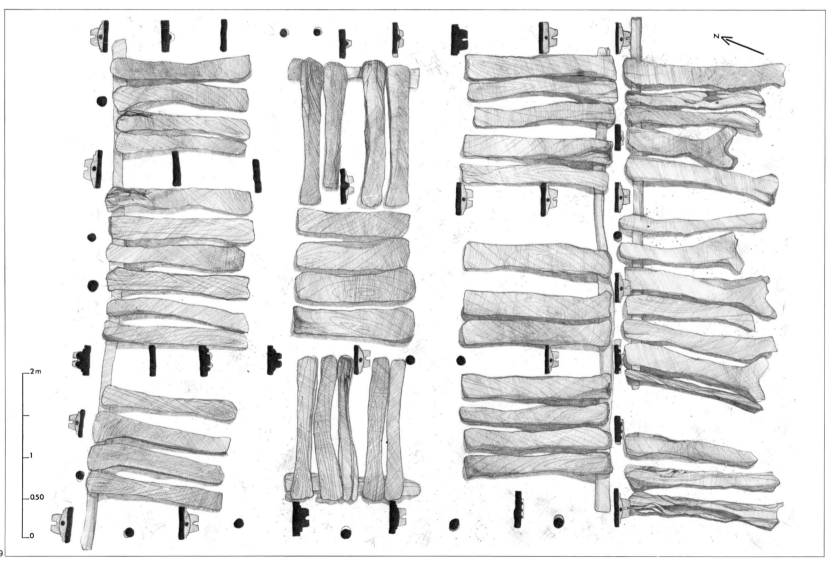

2m

1

0.50

0

199

man (testicles and penis) and seven, the sum of the two numbers is the number standing for copulation and procreation. The togu na as a building is reserved for the men while all the sculptures on the pillars dividing it up structurally are all female characters. This ratio and the repeated presence of the female sculptures in the togu na show the interpendence of man and woman.

The only two elements which might seem alien to this theory are two masks on the south side. Among the information collected was that of an ironical positioning of the gazelle (vilù) next to the woman, their behavior often being determined by the fact that they are both emotionally unstable. The *sirige* (house with several storeys) signifies amongst other things the house intended as a reference point for the family. So in this sense even these two symbols can be linked up with the man-woman hypothesis.

199. Plan of the togu na.
200. The south side.
201. The togu na, the "head" of the village.
202. The south side. The roof of millet straw weighs about 20 tons.
203, 204. The sculptures on the togu na in Youdiou are some of the oldest on the Séno plain (1500-1700?).

200

201

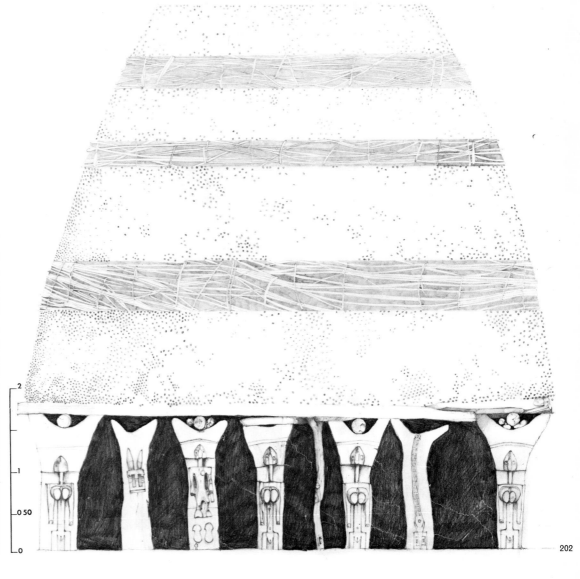
202

205

206

205. It is the job of the elders to make the basic decision involving community life. They reach and announce their decisions sitting in the togu na (the sitting position is considered ideal since the "water of the word" is smooth and calm).

206, 207. The pillars are made from a single piece of kilé wood (Prosopis africana). The actual support is 8 to 15 cms thick and the sculptures don't protrude more than 30 or 40 cms.

208, 209. The women are not allowed into the togu na and so they wait outside for the head of the togu na to announce the decisions to them.

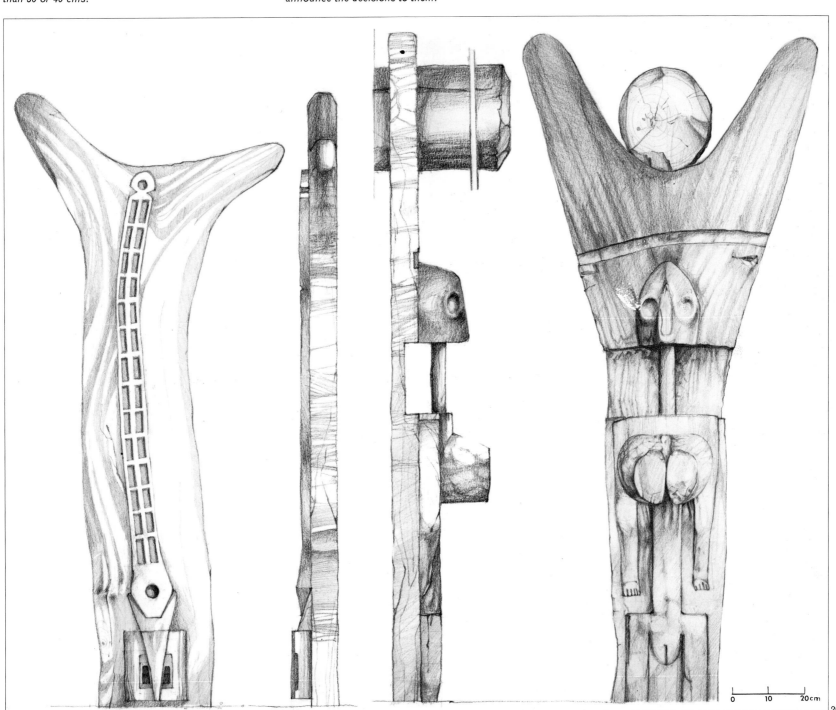

207

BENIEMA

Beniema ("to approach"). The togu na in the Perigourou district (tall tree of *Cassia nigricans*) is one of the few we analyzed with six pillars along the north and south sides. The number 6 is mythically connected to the Fox (Yourougou, the first son of Amma and the Earth) and divination. In the village of Pourali we watched them drawing a divining table: the diviner draws a rectangle on the sand divided up into six squares in which he puts some peanuts to attract the foxes which will come during the night. The tracks left by them will then be interpreted by the seer using a special code. There are, however, very few other indications that might lead us to the conclusion that this togu na is in some way directly linked with divination, though one of the pillars has drawings which we studied representing the lizard—a direct reference to the circumcised Fox, which could be worth going into more thoroughly. From a reading of the sculptures (somewhat fragmentary since many are missing) there emerged the further possibility of considering these figures as a reference to femininity.

The *valù* (antelope) mask is incited during the dance in the secret language (*sigi sò*) to frighten the women. The breasts and female figure are explicit references to woman; the pillar with the lizard and breasts on it may have yet another meaning besides the one suggested: that since the lizard represents the foreskin, it is the female part of the man which is thus removed through circumcision. The same treatment in the sculpture, almost osmosis of the lizard and breasts, emphasizes the concept of femininity.

210-212. The north side of the togu na at Perigorou and details of the pillars along this side.
213, 214. Detail and drawing of internal pillars.

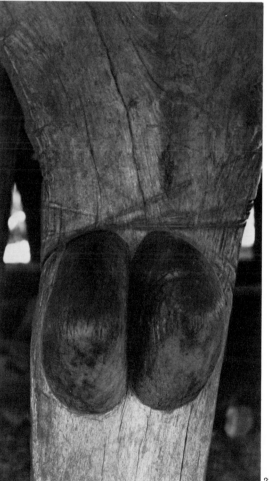

213

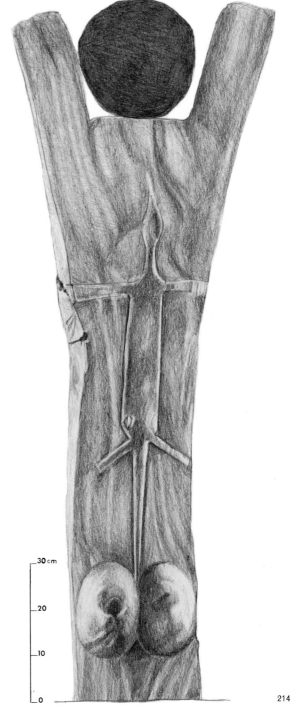

214

BENIEMA-NA

Beniema-na ("to come near to," "great" or "mother"). The area surrounding the village is a huge stretch of pastureland, luxuriant during the rainy season and arid in the dry season but sufficient for the basic needs of the herds. During this season the animals go to the villages to water at the many wells which have been dug in the area and which keep their water longer than the others as they are fed from the springs between the rocky belt and the plain. Beniema-na is enclosed by a hedge of thorny shrubs which prevents the animals from entering the village. The togu na in the two districts: Omorogara ("huge fetish") and Tomi ("settle nearby"), both lie outside the enclosure so that there is also constant contact between the villagers and the

215

216

204

herdsmen and shepherds. The togu na in Omorogara stands near the main well where the Peul nomads gather, and it is to them by tradition that the Dogon entrust the rearing of their animals. These meetings have always resulted in legendary tales of the animals in the undergrowth and some exceptional animal from the herds which in the figurative story become mythical in their appearance and behavior. Most of the tales refer to man's bloody victory over the animal when the latter, in a desperate violent reaction, in its attempt to escape death, injures or kills his assailants. The Dogon, who are always careful not to upset the balance in the nature surrounding them, see danger in these gestures of forced violence since the *nyama* (vital strength) of the animal wanders around to wreak vengeance on the killer. M. Griaule in his (*Masques Dogons*) claims this is the reason why the masks are carved in the shapes of animals, to exorcize the unrelenting evil forces. The togu na recalls, as we have often noticed, the symbol of fertility expressed both by the seven pillars and the female figures and exalted on the central pillar along the east side by the presence of the most important fertility symbol—two pairs of breasts representing twins. Here the concept of fertility is extended not only to the harvest (which is common among the Dogon) but also to the well-being of the herds which are, particularly in this village, an important instrument in survival. The *valù* masks, (an antelope which attacks the herds with its antlers) and the *bovidé* mask (the image of a fierce mythical ox, the head of a herd) are in all probability placed beside the fertility symbols so as to exorcize the danger to the herds and to make their vital strength benevolent.

215, 216. The togu na in Omorogara stands outside the fence surrounding the village near the place where the herds gather.

217. *The south side.*

218. *The well in the district of Omorogara has water even in the dry season and so is an obligatory stop for the Peul nomads who take their herds onto the Séno plain.*

219. *The east side.*

217

218

221. At the bottom of the forked wood deep scores have formed with the continual rubbing of the fibers used in rope-making.

222. The bovidé mask (the great mythical ox) exorcizes the evil forces which could kill the herds.

220. The valù mask (antelope horse which attacks the herds with its horns).

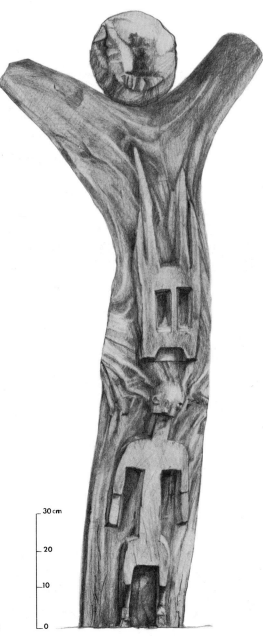

30 cm

20

10

0

220

221

223-225. Often when a pillar is broken or stolen it is replaced with another depicting the same subject as the previous sculpture (224); though different in style from the others (223-225) the thematic integrity is maintained.

223

224

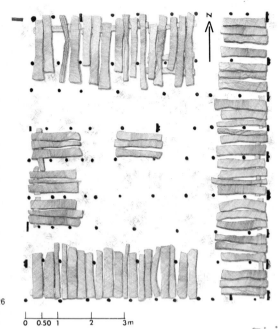

226

0 0.50 1 2 3m

The togu na in the Tomi ("settle nearby") district is, in area, the largest of those we examined. The traditional arrangement with the north-south axis parallel to the main side of the rectangle of the base is respected here but the main frontage is the one facing east looking onto the trail going from Koporokenié na to Woro.

This frontage is the only one which is complete in its sculptures (besides two pillars depicting female breasts, one in the centre and the other along the west side.) Certainly there must originally have been many others along the north and south sides but we were unable to get any information about this whatsoever; yet a missionary we met in Barapireli told us that when he had been there about ten years earlier the togu na had been complete and in perfect condition.

The vertical bearing structure of the building, despite much replacing of pillars,

has remained basically unchanged; however, the nine pillars on the frontage divide it into eight spaces inside. (Nine is the number referring to the word of wisdom and old age: eight is connected with the togu na itself since there were eight ancestors and there are eight elders who, in the judgments they pass "administer justice in the name of the eight ancestors who passed on their wisdom to them.") We believe that the positioning of the sculptures along the east side is purely incidental since all the carved pillars have been placed here to give a finished-off look to the togu na. On the roof at the point corresponding to the center of the main side hangs a bent stick, the *domolo*, particularly in evidence here on the togu na at Beniema na Tomi (together with a forked stick used by the rope makers.) This hook-shaped stick is the weapon used in fighting and throwing by the Dogon men and boys; this objects is inseparable from

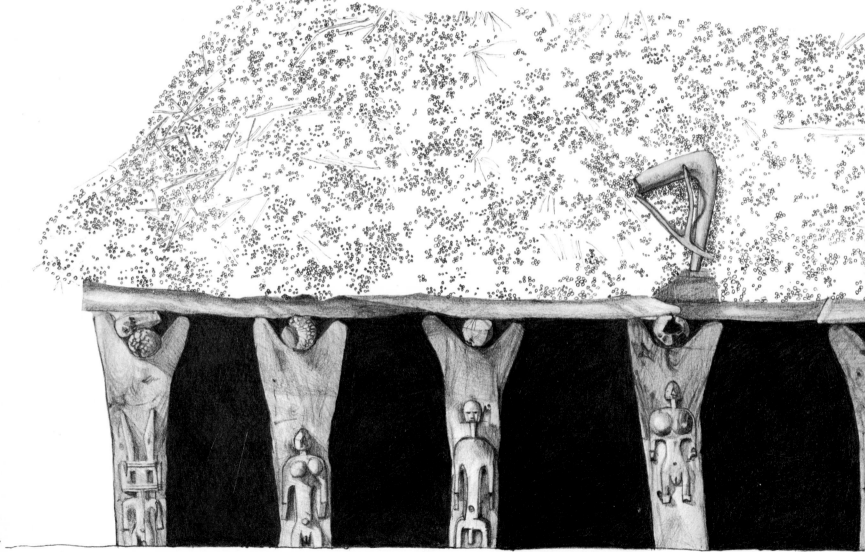

227

the men, so much so that it is considered the symbol of virility. The Dogon never leaves his *domolo* and at night he keeps it hanging from the beam above his bed. The shape of this object is the image of a star called the "hook star" the symbol both of the *domolo* itself and of the gesture made by Nommo when he came down from the sky in his ark and "hooked" the earth to take possession of it (*Le Renard Pâle*). The *domolo* is hung outside the togu na to underline the fact that the building is reserved for men (symbol of virility) and that fighting and quarrels must be left outside (symbolism of war) because the only words that can be uttered in the togu na are calm words of peace, wisdom and justice.

226. *Plan of the togu na in the district of Tomi.*
227. *The east side, drawing.*
228. *The east side.*

228

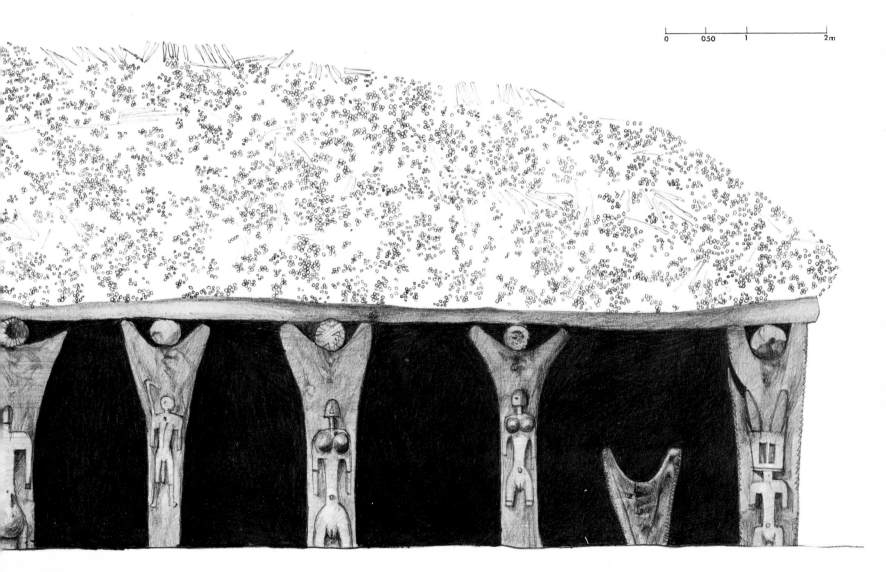

229-231. The only carved pillars left in this togu na have all been placed along the eastern side in a random order.

232. The hook-shaped stick hanging on the roof of the togu na is the domolo, *the ritual weapon, symbol of virility and war.*

230

229

231

233-235. *The soft wood seats that the men who work in the shade of the togu na sit on, take on the form of their body and the work done there.*

233

234

235

Woro (*volò*, "black thorn"—Having removed the thorns to enable you to settle here—) Myth attributes the origin of this very old village to the Monopouzo, descendants of the Dyon tribe. One of the founder of Amani's sons went into the earth and came out at the place where the village of Woro (or Wori) now stands. S. de Ganay says in *Les Dévises des Dogons:* "The Monopouzo were immortal; when they reached old age they used to dig inside the earth and came out rejuvenated; until the Wori group bought the death of Andoumboulou for the price of a seashell." (This version contrasts with the one stating that the first human death was that of Yougo-Dogourou. Woro is on the edge between the rocky belt and the plain, a position which made it easier for its inhabitants, during raids by enemy tribes, to reach the shelter offered by the rocky plateau more quickly, and as soon as danger had passed they were able to return to their land without having to abandon it for long periods. This led to the consolidation of deeper traditions which was not so easy for other villages on the Séno plain where they were compelled to emigrate from time to time and to adapt to the customs of the community to the relationships developed through contact with the inhabitants of the rocky belt. Although in structure, materials and sculpture the togu na conforms to the type generally found on the plain, the ones in Woro are created and used in the same spirit of tradition as those on the rocky belt. The nucleus of Woro, so enclosed and untouched, expresses in the togu na a series of very varied and complex symbols. Each one of the togu na in the three districts has five pillars along the main sides; it

should be noted that this number has a variety of basic meanings in Dogon life and mythology. In the togu na in the district of Gomonogara ("big family") there is considerable symbolic evidence in the sculptures and the signs; this is true to such an extent that it is possible to suggest an interpretation in a basic theory referring to fundamental elements of Dogon life. The *valù*, antelope, here depicted more as an animal than a mask (the mask never has a mouth and the openings for the eyes are carved as two vertical slits) could represent the constant contact man has with life in the undergrowth. A thorough research into the symbolism of locks is being carried out at the Musée de L'Homme in Paris by G. Calame-Griaule, who with a group of scholars puts forward the theory that one of the sexual symbolic meanings which might be attributed to this object is that of marriage. The Grecian vertical lines on the base of the pillar could be: the undulating one on the left, the poetic word and song; the one on the right, sharp and regular, the normal calmly spoken word.

The placing one above the other of the lock, breasts and double placenta is a synthesis of the perfect union between man and woman: marriage—fertility—birth of twins (the double placenta). The large horizontal Grecian line is identifiable as the symbol of water. The essentiality of the subjects depicted is organic with one of the simplest meanings of the number five, that of being the basic number in counting (five fingers on each hand) and corresponding to the

236. The north side in the district of Gomonogara.
237. Anndou, the head of the togu na.

WORO

238. Greek frets symbolizing water.

239. The antelope—not the mask but the animal in the undergrowth; the lock representing marriage; vertical Greek frets, the diagrams of poetry and song.

240. Marriage in its fulfillment of maximum fertility, the twin birth (double placenta).

238

239

241

242

days in the week (the basic cycle in Dogon life.) The different sculptures in the Woro togu na, in the Lei district ("second") whether analyzed one by one or with an overall significance seem to go to make up the mythology of genealogy and the first generations. On the east side there are only two carved pillars left. Regarding the footprints left by the sandals the popular theory is that they are Amma's footprints (God, the supreme being) but other informants with a deeper mythological knowledge told us that these are the footmarks of Nommo (the unity of the two twins created by Amma who represent order and well-being in contrast to Yourougou—Fox—the symbol of disorder and evil) when for the first time he set foot on earth disembarking from the ark which had brought him from the skies opened up by Amma till he reached the banks of Lake Débo (in the area of the Niger to the north of Mopti). We believe that this might well be the most likely version since in many other villages, where the footprints were attributed to Amma, they were in fact footmarks placed side by side, whilst these in the togu na at Woro in the district of Lei show, by their position, the action of walking as Nommo did when he took possession of the earth.

On the second pillar is carved the outline of the mythical genealogy showing Amma as the first being, the first three creatures: Yourougou and the Nommo twins, the first eight ancestors each one of them having a twin of the opposite sex. On the opposite west side of the togu na four of the five pillars have female sculptures on them, the

243

fifth has been replaced recently, but from information given to us it would appear to have also had a female figure on it. These five female figures here go to represent the succession of the first five generations forming a complete genealogical cycle with the Dogon division of generations.
Other important signs which may help in forming a hypothesis concerning the symbolism referring to Dogon mythology and the first creatures are two sculptures on the inside pillars of the togu na. One is a complete synthesis between the Fox, circumcision, the turning of the foreskin into a lizard, the symbol of femininity and impurity; the other depicts the Fox emerging from his mother, Earth, after having committed incest with her. Particularly effective, representatively speaking, is the idea of substituting the symbolic element (the earth) with the real element. Thus the link between the Fox and Nommo who circumcised him is completed as is also the link between Nommo and Amma, the latter having sacrificed him to reestablish order in the chaotic universe. Finally the resurrection of Nommo five days after his death suggests the examination of the number five as the basis of an interdependent relationship between creation-purification and the first Dogon generations.

241. The west side in the district of Lei.
242. The east side in the district of Lei.
243. The south-west corner in the district of Lei.
244. The footprints left by Nommo's sandals when he came down to earth.

244

245, 246. Close-ups of the west side.

247. The mythical genealogy of the Dogon.

248

248-250. *The patriarchal structure upholding the Dogon world holds woman in great esteem for she is often depicted in the togu na as the fundamental element in supporting the building, symbol of balance and justice.*
251. *The lizard,* nay, *symbol of femininity and impurity.*

250

249

252. *The Fox—Yourougou—comes out of the earth after having committed incest.*

251

252

253. *Detail on one of the pillars depicting the first three creatures in Dogon mythology.*

254. *This recent sculpture is an attempt at a realistic representation of a human figure, very different from the abstraction and hyperbole in the older sculptures.*

253

254

The third district in Woro is Konié-nu ("huge termite which comes out of the earth after the rain," the Dogon children eat it). The sign-symbols appearing on the pillars of the togu na in this district are difficult—almost impossible—to connect up with each other, and no help was offered to us in finding a coherent explanation of the reading. The sculpture on the east side could be, reading from top to bottom, a succession of events in myth and in real life which are hypothetically connected: the Fox's teeth responsible for disorder, Amman's footprints by means of which order is brought back to the universe, man and the lock at his feet which is emblematic of a deep and fertile relationship both with the earth and with woman whose image

255

256

appears along with the relative symbols of complete fertility included in the sculptures on the lateral pillars. The presence of a lock sculptured on an internal pillar, isolated unconnected to other symbols, recalls the image of the barn on the door of which it can usually be seen; this again suggests the theme of fertility. (Incidentally we should like to point out that in *Le Renard Pâle* by M. Griaule and G. Dieterlen, page 419, in the description of the ark of the universe, divided into sixty rooms, which transported all beings and things, the barn is situated in room number five.)

This numerical reference, of which we received no confirmation in the village, could, however, be connected with the number five which we pointed out as being an element in the link between the three togu na of Woro.

255-257. *The togu na in the district of Konié-nu photographed from the path which links the village with the well and the place where the millet is threshed.*
258. *A close-up of the east side.*

257

259. *The lock on the barn as an image of fertility.*

260, 261. *The ideogram represents the relationship between myth and reality, between disorder and order, between god and man and between man, woman and earth.*

259

260

NIONGONO

(A man arrived at this place he didn't know. Feeling frightened he backed away walking on tiptoe; another man arrived and said to him: "Don't be afraid; settle here!") Niongono is part of a small group of fortified villages separated from the rest of the Dogon territory in the area south-west of Bandjagara as far as Baboje. Isolated rocky hillocks stick up from the plain, and the villages are perched on them. The reason for these settlements completely cut off from the region all the Dogon villages,

are situated in from Bandjagara in the north-east as far as Douentza, lies exclusively in the struggles which the village of Bandjagara underwent throughout the nineteenth century. Particularly cruel and oppressive was the Toucouleurs domination (Islamic tribe of Peul origin) led by El-Hadj Omar. The figure of this chief is legendary for on the pretext of waging a religious war he raided and exterminated every Dogon village surrounding Bandjagara. Prevented by the raiders from reaching the Dogon territory, these small isolated groups took refuge in the most inaccessible parts of the area. The village of Niongono, situated on the top of a horse-shoe shaped rock, is defended by double walls at the foot of the hill, by a series of natural ramparts formed by the rocky terracing and the structural layout of the buildings. In contrast to the general kind of Dogon dwelling unit which is divided into family units, at Niongono a 15-foot wall completely surrounds each of the districts in the village. Only inside this protective wall do the houses and barns take on the dimensions of single-family habitations. Access to the fortified village can only be gained through a narrow doorway so a constant check can be kept on the place. The many attacks suffered by the inhabitants have made them behave defensively even though the reasons for doing so have disappeared and they now live in voluntary isolation. Their world is cut off and their exasperated attempt to remain self-sufficient (in the past any kind of contact with the outside world only caused them to suffer violence and oppression) means that they still behave extremely diffidently when approached by any outsider. Our contact with the village had to be established in different stages after submitting to a series of checks carried out to ascertain out intentions and the reasons for our interest. Our conversations with the old men of the village took place in the togu na, the only buildings outside the protective wall. The togu na are built entirely in stone and they are almost circular in their layout, half of the perimeter being in continuous walling and the other half having pillars wich allow ventilation and serve as the entrance ways. The role of the togu na in these villages is the traditional one—the men's house—the house of words—and meeting place for the different districts (the inhabitants have to cross the walls to reach the togu na or another district): besides it is the look-out post and checkpoint for the entrance through the double walls. Finally it is a "filter" through which a stranger's word must pass, be discussed and assessed before he is allowed to enter the inner nucleus of the village, thus further underlining the character of truth, integrity and justice of the words uttered within the togu na.

262, 263. The togu na in the districts of Niongono, outside the surrounding walls act as look-out posts and "filter."

Step into the footmarks of your ancestors. Tradition may weaken but cannot disappear.

(from a Dogon prayer recorded by G. Dieterlen).

BIBLIOGRAPHY

General Information

Adande Alexandre, *Masques africains*, in « Notes Africaines, » No. 51, Dakar, 1951.

Arnaud Robert, *Notes sur les montagnards Habé des cercles de Bandjagara et de Hombori (Soudan Français)*, in « Revue d'éthnographie et des traditions populaires, » No. 2, Paris, 1921.

Baumann H., Westermann Dietrich, *Les peuples et les civilisations de l'Afrique. Les langues et l'éducation*, Payot, Paris, 1948.

Brasseur Paul, *Bibliographie générale du Mali*, Institut d'Afrique noire, Dakar, 1964.

Cornevin Robert et Marianne, *Histoire de l'Afrique (dès origines à la deuxième guerre mondiale)*, Payot, Paris, 1964.

Davidson Basil, *The Africans. An Entry to Cultural History*, Longmans-Green & Co., London, 1969.

Delafosse Maurice, *Haut Sénégal-Niger (Soudan Français). Les pays, les peuples, les langues, l'histoire, les civilisations*, Larose, Paris, 1912.

Deschamps Hubert, *Histoire général de l'Afrique noire*, Presses Universitaires de France, Paris, 1970-1971.

Desplanges Louis, *Le Plateau Central Nigérien*, Larose, Paris, 1907.

N'Diaye Bokar, *Groupes ethniques au Mali*, Editions Populaires, Bamako, 1970.

Dieterlen Germaine, *Les Ames des Dogon*, Institut d'Ethnologie, Paris, 1941.

Dieterlen Germaine, *Notes sur les migrations soudanaises au Ghana*, in « Africa Notes and News, » XXVII, No. 3, London, 1957.

Dieterlen Germaine, *Contribution à la préhistoire de la région du lac Debo*, Record of the VI International Conference of Anthropological and Ethnographical Sciences, No. 11, Paris, 1960.

Dieterlen Germaine, *Dictionnaire des civilisations africaines*, Fernand Hazan, Paris, 1968.

Frobenius Leo, *Kulturtypen aus dem Westsudan*, J. Perthes, Gotha, 1910.

Frobenius Leo, *Dämonen des Sudans*, in « Revue Atlantis, » No. 5, Jena, 1922.

Frobenius Leo, *Das unbekannte Afrika*, Oscar Beck, München, 1923.

Frobenius Leo, *Dichten und Denken in Sudan*, in « Revue Atlantis, » No. 7, Jena, 1924.

Frobenius Leo, *Erzählungen aus dem Westsudan*, in « Revue Atlantis, » No. 8, Jena, 1925.

Griaule Marcel, *La mission Dakar-Djibouti dans son rapport avec les études éthnologiques et archéologiques*, in « Revue de Synthèse, » No. 3, Paris, 1931.

Griaule Marcel, *Mission Dakar-Djibouti, rapport général*, in « Journal de la Société des Africanistes », No. 11, Paris, 1932.

Griaule Marcel, *Mission Dakar-Djibouti. Les résultats*, in « Aetiopica, » I, New York, 1933.

Griaule Marcel, *La mission Dakar-Djibouti*, in « L'Afrique française, » Paris, 1933.

Griaule Marcel, *Rapport sur la IV mission Griaule 1936-37*, in « La géographie, » LXVII, Paris, 1937.

Griaule Marcel, *Notes sur les Dogon du Soudan français*, in « Journal de la S.d.A., » Paris, 1941.

Griaule Marcel, *La civilisation Dogon, survivance d'une Afrique disparue*, in « Le Monde illustré, » Paris, 1947.

Griaule Marcel, *L'inconnue noire*, in « Présence africaine, » Paris-Dakar, 1947.

Griaule Marcel, *Connaissance de l'homme noir*, in « Rencontres internationales de Genève, » La Baconnière, Neuchâtel, 1951.

Griaule Marcel, *Les Dogon*, in « La documentation française, » Paris, 1952 (English edition *African Worlds*, Oxford University Press, London, New York, Toronto, 1954).

Heim A., *Negro Sahara*, Hans Huber, Bern, 1934.

Labouret Henri, *Histoire des noirs d'Afrique*, Presses Universitaires de France, Paris, 1950.

Leiris Michel, *L'Afrique fantôme*, Gallimard, Paris, 1934.

Leiris Michel, *Les Dogon, peuplade du Soudan français*, Agenzia Internazionale Fides, Roma, 1953.

Lhote Henri, *Les Habès, La Terre et la Vie*, Paris, 1933.

Maquet Jaques, *Les civilisations noires*, Marabout Université, Veviers, 1966.

Palau Marti Montserrat, *Les Dogon*, Monographies ethnologiques africaines P.U.F., Paris-London, 1957.

Van Ravenstijn P. Paul, *Sur les bords du Niger, les Dogon*, in « Grands Lacs », No. 5, Namur, 1953.

Wauthier Claude, *L'Afrique des Africains*, Editions du Seuil, Paris, 1964.

Environment

Annuaire statistique de l'Union française-outre-mer, 1939/49, Imprimerie Nationale de France, 2 vols., Paris, 1951.

Daveau Suzanne, *Recherches morphologiques sur la région de Bandjagara*, Institut français de l'Afrique noire, Dakar, 1959.

Dieterlen Germaine, *Emploi des plantes ichthyotossiques pour la pêche chez les Dogon de Sanga*, in « Notes Africaines, » No. 56, Dakar, 1952.

Gautier E. F., *L'Afrique noire occidentale. Esquisse des cadres géografiques*, Larose, Paris, 1935.

Griaule Marcel, *La région des falaises du Niger*, in « Revue d'Afrique, » No. 13, Paris, 1935.

Griaule Marcel, *Tanières des crocodiles dans les falaises nigériennes*, in « Journal de la S.d.A., » No. 11, Paris, 1941.

Griaule Marcel, *Notes biogéographiques sur les falaises de Bandjagara* (summarized report of the meetings of the Société de Biogéographie), Paris, 1941.

Griaule Marcel, *Les mammifères dans la région des Dogon*, in « Mammalia, » No. 5, Paris, 1941.

Griaule Marcel, *Classification des insectes chez les Dogon*, in « Journal de la S.d.A., » No. XXXI, Paris, 1961.

Jaeger P. et Winkound, *Premier contact avec la flore et la végétation du plateau de Bandjagara*, in « Bullettin de l'IFAN, » series A XXIV, Dakar, 1962.

Serpokrylov S., *Carte géologique du plateau de Bandjagara et de la plaine du Gondo*, Service géologique de l'A.O.F., Dakar, 1934.

Le Soudan français, Agence de la France d'outre-mer, Paris, 1952.

Weuleresse Jacques, *L'Afrique noire*, A. Fayard & Co., Paris, 1934.

Map of West Africa (1: 200,000): Bandjagara (1955), Bambara-Maundé (1959), Douentza (1960), Hombori (1959), Gao (1959), Gourma-Rharous (1959), Mopti (1956), Ouahigouya (1955), San (1956), Segou (1956), Tougan (1955), Ké-Macina (1955). Institut National Geographique.

Michelin Map No. 153, North-West Africa, (1: 4,000,000), Ed. Pneu. Michelin, Paris, 1969.

Maps of West Africa (1: 5,500,000), Edward Stanford LTD, London, 1962.

Social Life

Beart Ch., *Jeux et jouets de l'ouest africain*, IFAN, Dakar, 1955.

Calame Griaule G., *Le vêtement dogon, confection et usage*, in « Journal de la S.d.A., » No. 21, Paris, 1951.

Deschamps Hubert, *L'éveil politique africain*, Presses Universitaires de France, Paris, 1952.

Dieterlen Germaine, *Parenté et mariage chez les Dogon*, in « Africa, » No. 26, London, 1956.

Dieterlen Germaine, *Mythe et organisation sociale au Soudan français*, in « Journal de la S.d.A., » No. XXV, Paris, 1955.

Dieterlen Germaine, *L'alimentation dogon*, Cahiers of African Studies, Paris, 1960.

Diougoudie Dolo, *Monographie d'un village: Sanga*, in « L'éducation africaine », No. 93, Gorée, 1936.

Griaule Marcel, *Le chasseur du 20 octobre* (funeral ceremonies of the Dogon of Bandjagara), in « Minotaure, » No. 2, Paris, 1933.

Griaule Marcel, *Jeux dogons*, Institut d'Ethnologie, Paris, 1938.

Griaule Marcel, *Remarques sur le mécanisme du sacrifice dogon*, in « Journal de la S.d.A., » Paris, 1940.

Griaule Marcel, *Remarques sur l'oncle utérin au Soudan*, Cahiers internationaux de sociologie, Paris, 1954.

Griaule Marcel, *Rôle spirituel et social de la femme dans la société soudanaise traditionnelle*, in « Diogène, » No. 37, Paris, 1962.

Ganay Solange, *Les Ogol, plan parcellaire provisoire*, Documents of the Giaule expeditions, Paris, 1936.

Ganay Solange, *Instruments aratoires et herminettes dogon*, in « Notes Africaines, » No. 60, Dakar, 1953.

Leiris Michel, *Dances funéraires dogon*, in « Minotaure, » No. 1, Paris, 1933.

Leiris Michel, Schaeffner André, *Les rites de circoncision chez les Dogon de Sanga*, in « Journal de la S.d.A., » Paris, 1936.

Lifchitz Deborah, Paulme Denise, *Les noms individuels chez les Dogon*, in « Mémoires de l'IFAN, » No. 6, Dakar, 1953.

Malroux, *Differents rapports concernant l'enseignement chez les Dogon*, Paris, 1953.

Minelli E., *Usi e costumi del Sudan francese. Il rito della caverna per gli spiriti Yapilu*, in « Le vie d'Italia e del mondo, » No. 4, Milano, 1936.

Ortoli Henri, *Le décès d'une femme enceinte chez les Dogon de Bandjagara*, in « Bullettin IFAN, » Paris, 1941.

Ortoli Henri, *Les rites de la maternité chez les Dogon de Bandjagara*, in « Bullettin IFAN, » No. 3, Dakar, 1941.

Ouane Ibrahim Mamadou, *Notes sur les Dogon au Soudan français (annoté per M. Griaule)*, in « Journal de la S.d.A., » No. 11, Paris, 1941.

Paulme Denise, *La communauté taisible chez les Dogon*, Domat-Montchrestien, Paris, 1937.

Paulme Denise, *Organisation sociale des Dogon*, Domat-Montchrestien, Paris, 1940.

Religion, Cosmogony, Customs

Adler A., Cartry M., *La transgression et sa dérision*, in « L'homme, » July-September 1971.

Amman Abdl el Qader, *Moeurs et coutumes indigènes. Le paganisme des Habbé*, in « La revue indigène, » No. 15, Paris, 1920.

Bruil Abbé Henri, *L'Afrique préhistorique*, Cahiers d'art, Paris, 1950.

Calame-Griaule G., *Culture et humanisme chez les Dogon*, Research and debates of the Centre Catholique des intellectuels français, Paris, 1958.

Deschamps Hubert, *Les religions de l'Afrique noire*, Presses Universitaires de France, Paris, 1954.

Dieterlen Germaine, *Le duge signe d'alliance chez les Dogon de Sanga*, in « Bulletin du Comité d'études historiques et scientifiques de l'A.O.F., » No. 21, Paris, 1938.

Dieterlen Germaine, *Mécanisme de l'impureté chez les Dogon*, in « Journal de la S.d.A., » No. 17, Paris, 1947.

Dieterlen Germaine, *Symbolisme des tambours soudanais*, Richard Masse, Paris, 1955.

Dieterlen Germaine, *Rôle du silure, Clarias senegalensis, dans la procréation au Soudan*, Afrikanistische Studien, Berlin, 1955.

Dieterlen Germaine, *Symbolisme d'un temple totémique soudanais*, Report of the Conference on cosmic symbolism of religions monuments, No. XIV, Paris, 1957.

Dieterlen Germaine, *Notes sur les tambours des calebasses en Afrique occidentale*, in « Journal de la S.d.A., » No. XXX, Paris, 1960.

Dieterlen Germaine, *Religions africaines et culture en Afrique occidentale*, in « Présence Africaine, » April, Abidjan-Paris, 1961.

Dieterlen Germaine, *Notes sur le totémisme dogon*, in « L'Homme, » January-April, Paris, 1963.

Dieterlen Germaine, *La notion de personne et la réincarnation chez les Dogon*, Report of the Strasbourg Conference, Strasbourg, 1963.

Dieterlen Germaine, *Blasons et emblèmes totémiques des Dogon*, Catalogue of the exhibition « Emblèmes, Totems, Blason, » Musèe Guimet, Paris, 1964.

Dieterlen G., Ganay S., *Le génie des eaux chez les Dogon*, in « Miscellanea Africana, » No. V, Parìs, 1942.

Ganay Solange, *Note sur le culte du lébé chez les Dogon du Soudan français*, in « Journal de la S.d.A., » No. 7, Paris, 1937.

Ganay Solange, *Rôle protecteur de certaines peintures rupestres du Soudan français*, in « Journal de la S.d.A., » No. 10, Paris, 1940.

Ganay Solange, *Les devises des Dogon*, Institut d'Ethnologie, Paris, 1941.

Ganay Solange, *Le Binou Yébéné*, Librairie orientaliste Paul Genthner, Paris, 1942.

Ganay Solange, *Le génie des eaux chez les Dogon, les Kouroumba, les Sara*, Compte rendu de l'Institut français d'Anthropologie, Paris, 1949.

Griaule Marcel, *Peintures rupestres du Soudan français*, in « Revue de Synthèse, » No. 3, Dec., Paris, 1934.

Griaule Marcel, *Peintures rupestres du Soudan français et leur sens religieux*, Report of the first session of the International Conference of Anthropological and Ethnological Sciences, Royal Anthropological Institute, London, 1934.

Griaule Marcel, *Rites relatifs aux peintures rupestres dans le Soudan français*, Report of the meetings of the Société de Biogéographie, n. 95, Paris, 1934.

Griaule Marcel, *Le curieux totémisme des Dogon de Sanga*, Excerpt from « Le Mois, » Sept.-Oct., Paris, 1935.

Griaule Marcel, *Le culte du lamantin dans les falaises nigériennes*, Summarized report of the meetings of the Société de Biogéographie, No. 13, Paris, 1936.

Griaule Marcel, *Blasons totémiques dogon*, in « Journal de la S.d.A., » No. 7, Paris, 1937.

Griaule Marcel, *Notes sur la divination par le chacal (population Dogon de Sanga)*, in « Bulletin du Comité d'études historiques et scientifiques de l'Afrique occidentale, » Jan.-June, No. XX, Paris, 1937.

Griaule Marcel, *Masques dogon*, Institut d'Ethnologie, Paris, 1938.

Griaule Marcel, *Notes complémentaires sur les masques dogon*, in « Journal de la S.d.A., » No. 10, Paris, 1940.

Griaule Marcel, *La personnalité chez les Dogon*, in « Journal de psychologie normale et pathologique, » No. 37, Paris, 1940-1941.

Griaule Marcel, *Couples joumelées au Soudan*, in « Notes Africaines, » No. 36, Dakar, 1947.

Griaule Marcel, *Déscente du troisième Verbe chez les Dogon du Soudan*, Extrait de « Psyché », No. 13, Nov.-Dec., Paris, 1947.

Griaule Marcel, *Mythe de l'organisation du monde chez les Dogon du Soudan*, in « Psyché », No. 2, Paris, 1947.

Griaule Marcel, *Nouvelles recherches sur la notion de personne chez les Dogon*, in « Journal de psychologie normale et pathologique, » No. 40 Paris, 1947.

Griaule Marcel, *Valeur symbolique du vêtement dogon*, in « Revue d'esthétique, » No. 1, Paris, 1947.

Griaule Marcel, *L'alliance cathartique*, in « Africa, » No. 18, London, 1948.

Griaule Marcel, *L'arche du monde chez les populations nigériennes*, in « Journal de la S.d.A., » No. 18, Paris, 1948.

Griaule Marcel, *Dieu d'eau*, Editions du Chêne, Paris, 1948.

Griaule Marcel, *La harpe-luth des Dogon*, in « Journal de la S.d.A., » No. 20, Paris, 1950.

Griaule Marcel, *Art et symbole en Afrique noire*, Zodiaque cahiers de l'Atelier du Coeur Meurtri, No. 2/5, Paris, 1951.

Griaule Marcel, *Signes graphiques soudanais*, Hermann & Co., Paris, 1951.

Griaule Marcel, *Les Dogon*, Explorations outre-mer, Paris, 1952.

Griaule Marcel, *Le savoir des Dogon*, in « Journal de ? S.d.A., » No. 22, Paris, 1952.

Griaule Marcel, *Nouvelles remarques sur la harpe-luth des Dogon*, in « Journal de la S.d.A., » No. XXIV, Paris, 1954.

Guerrier Eric, *Essai sur la cosmogonie des Dogon, L'arche du Nommo*, Laffont, Paris, 1975.

Labouret Henri, *Sacrifices humaines en Afrique occidentale*, in « Journal de la S.d.A. ,» No. 11, Paris, 1941.

Leiris Michel, *Masques dogon*, in « Minotaure, » No. 2, Paris, 1933.

Leiris Michel, *Objets rituels dogon*, in « Minotaure, » No. 2, Paris, 1933.

Leiris Michel, *Rhombes dogon et dogon pignari*, in « Bulletin du Musée d'Ethnographie du Trocadero, » No. 7, Paris, 1934.

Leiris Michel, *Bois rituels des falaises*, Cahiers d'art, No. 11, Paris, 1936.

Leiris Michel, *La notion de awa chez les Dogon*, in « Journal de la S.d.A. ,» No. XI, Paris, 1941.

Lifchitz Deborah, *Devinettes et proverbes dogon*, in « Revue de Folklore français et de Folklore colonial, » No. 9, Paris, 1938.

Lifchitz Deborah, *Les formules propitiatoires chez les Dogon des falaises de Bandjagara*, in « Journal de la S.d.A., » No. 8, Paris, 1938.

Lifchitz Deborah, *La littérature orale chez les Dogon du Soudan français*, in « Africa, » No. 13, London, 1940.

Lifchitz Deborah, Paulme Denise, *Les animaux dans le folklore Dogon*, in « Revue de folklore français et de folklore colonial, » No. 7, Paris, 1936.

Michaut Pierre, *Les danses des Dogon, d'après un film de Griaule*, in « L'Opinion », Sept., Paris, 1938.

Michel-Jones F., *Dualisme, gémelléité, bisexualité et ambivalence chez les Dogon*, Paris, (1973) not yet in print.

Palau Marti Montserrat, *Ogo et binukedine, quelques considérations sur les cultes du Lébé*, in « Revue d'histoire des religions », No. 159, Paris, 1960.

Paulme Denise, *La divination par les chacals chez les Dogon de Sanga*, in « Journal de la S.d.A., » No. 7, Paris, 1937.

Paulme Denise, *Parenté à plaisenterie et alliance par le sang en Afrique occidentale*, in « Africa, » No. 12, London, 1939.

Paulme Denise, *Sur quelques rites de purification des Dogon*, in « Journal de la S.d.A., » No. 10, Paris, 1940.

Paulme Denise, Lifchitz Deborah, *Les fêtes des semailles en 1935 chez les Dogon de Sanga*, in « Journal de la S.d.A., » No. 6, Paris, 1936.

Schaeffner André, *Peintures rupestres de Songo*, in « Minotaure, » No. 2, Paris, 1933.

Schaeffner André, *Musique, danse et danse des masques dans une société nègre*, II International Conference of Aesthetics and Art Science, Paris, 1937.

Tiemoko Traore, *Nomination d'un Hogon ou grand chef des fétiches dans le canton de Inde (subdivision de Bandjagara)*, in « Bulletin d'information et renseignements, » No. 187, Dakar, 1938.

Zahan D., *Aperçu sur la pensée théogonique des Dogon*, in « Cahiers internationaux de sociologie », No. 6, Paris, 1949.

Zahan D., *Notes sur le luth dogon*, in « Journal de la S.d.A. », No. 20, Paris, 1950.

Zahan D., Ganay Solange, *Etudes sur la cosmologie des Dogon et des Bambara du Soudan français*, in « Africa, » No. 21, London, 1951.

Building Techniques

Brasseur Gérard, *Les établissements humains au Mali*, in « Bulletin de l'IFAN », Dakar, 1968.

Calame-Griaule G., *Notes sur l'habitation du plateau central nigérien*, in « Bulletin de l'IFAN », July, Dakar, 1955.

Haan Herman, *I Dogon*, in « Edilizia Moderna, » No. 89/90, Milano, 1967.

Oliver Paul, *Shelter in Africa*, Barrie & Jenkins, London, 1971.

Linguistics

Bertho P.J., *La place des dialectes dogon (dogo) de la falaise de Bandjagara parmi les autres groupes linguistiques de la zone soudanaise*, in « Bulletin de l'IFAN », No. 15, Dakar, 1953.

Calame-Griaule Geneviève, *Diversité linguistique et organisation social chez les Dogon du Soudan français*, in « Notes africaines, » No. 55, Dakar, 1952.

Calame-Griaule Geneviève, *Les moqueries de village au Soudan français*, in « Notes africaines », No. 61, Dakar, 1954.

Calame-Griaule Geneviève, *Esothérisme et fabulation au Soudan*, in « Bulletin de l'IFAN, » No. 2, Dakar, 1954.

Calame-Griaule Geneviève, *Les dialectes dogon*, in « Africa », London, 1956.

Calame-Griaule Geneviève, *Ethnologie et Language. La parole chez les Dogon*, Gallimard, Paris, 1965.

Calame-Griaule Geneviève, *Dictionnaire dogon. Langue et civilisation*, Klincksieck, Paris, 1968.

Holas B., *Encore un problème de l'orthographie des termes vernaculaires*, in « Notes africaines », No. 62, Dakar, 1954.

Jones F., Michel P.A., *Analyse stylistique de quelques oeuvres du pays dogon suivi d'un essai d'analyse sémantique*, Institut d'Ethnologie, Archives et Documents, microéditions n. 7082830.

Leiris Michel, *La langue de la société des hommes chez les Dogon de Sanga*, in « L'Anthropologie », No. 48, Paris, 1938.

Leiris Michel, *La langue secrète des Dogon de Sanga*, in « Travaux et mémoires de l'Institut d'Ethnologie », No. 50, Paris, 1948.

Kervan P. Marcel, *Les parlers dogon*, Department of African Linguistics of the Faculté des Lettres et de Sciences Humaines de l'Université de Dakar, Dakar, 1969.

Anthropology and Ethno-psychiatry

Devereux Georges, *Essais d'éthnopsychiatrie générale*, Gallimard, Paris, 1970.

Dieterlen Germaine, *La personnalité chez les Dogon*, in « Anthropologie, » No. XLIX, Paris, 1939.

Dieterlen Germaine, *Correspondances cosmo-biologiques chez les Soudanais*, in « Journal de psychologie normale et pathologique, » No. 3, Le Havre, 1950.

Dieterlen Germaine, *L'aggressivité dans la cosmologie de certaines sociétés d'Afrique de l'ouest*, Report of a Conference held at the Institut des relations humaines, Paris, 1963.

Griaule Marcel, *Introduction méthodologique*, in « Minotaure » (Special issue dedicated to the Mission Dakar-Djibouti, Paris, 1933.

Griaule Marcel, *La personnalité chez les Dogon*, in « Journal de psycologie normale et pathologique, » No. XXXVII, Paris, 1940-1941.

Parin P., Morgenthaler, Parin-Matthey G., *Les blancs pensent trop*, Payot, Paris, 1966.

Art

African Folktales and Sculpture (Introduction by Paul Racin), Bolligen Foundation Inc., New York, 1966.

Arts connus et méconnus de l'Afrique noire (Collection Paul Tishman - Introduction by Jaqueline Delange), Musée de l'Homme, Paris, 1966.

Arts primitifs dans les ateliers d'artistes, Musée de l'Homme, Paris, 1967.

Bravmann René A., *West African Sculpture*, of Washington, University Press, Washington, 1970.

Calame Blaise, Calame-Griaule G., *Scènes de la vie Dogon*, Club de la qualité, Paris, 1957.

Chefs d'oeuvre du Musée de l'Homme (Introduction by Roger Heim), Caisse Nationale des Monuments Historiques, Paris, 1965.

Colloque sur l'art nègre, Société Africaine de Culture, Dakar, 1967.

Delange Jaqueline (préface de Michel Leiris), *Arts et peuples de l'Afrique noire*, Gallimard, Paris, 1967.

Fagg William, *African Tribal Images*, Museum of Art.

The Katerine Reswich Collection, Cleveland, 1968.

Griaule Marcel, *Arts de l'Afrique noire* (photographs by Marcel Sougez now at the Musée de l'Homme), Edition du Chêne, Paris, 1947.

Griaule Marcel, *Les symbols des arts africaines*, in « Presence africaine, » No. 10/11, Paris-Dakar, 1951.

Griaule Marcel, *Systèmes graphiques des Dogon*, in « L'Homme, » No. III, Paris, 1951.

Kjersmeier Carl, *Centres de style de la sculpture africaine*, Edition Albert Morancé, Paris, 1935-38, 4 volumes.

Leiris Michel, Delange Jaqueline, *Afrique noire, la création plastique*, Gallimard, Paris, 1967.

Laude Jean, *African Art of the Dogon*, The Brooklyn Museum ,New York, 1973.

Lem F.H., *Sculptures soudanaises*, Arts et Métiers Graphiques, Paris, 1948.

Leuzinger Elsy, *Afrika*, *Kunst der Negervölker*, Holle Verlag, Baden-Baden, 1959.

Meauze Pierre, *L'art nègre*, Editions Hachette, Paris, 1967.

Rudofsky Bernard, *Architecture Without Architects*, The Museum of Modern Art, New York, 1965.

Segy Stanislas, *African Names and Sculpture*, in « Acta Tropica, » No. 10, Basel, 1953.

Wassing R.S., *L'Art de l'Afrique noire*, Bibliothèque des Arts, Office du livre, Paris, 1969.

References and Comparisons with Other African Peoples

Brasseur Gérard, *Peul et Rimaibé du Séno de Bandjagara*, International Conference of West African Studies Abidjan, 1953.

Brevie J., *Islamisme contre « naturisme » au Soudan français*, Edition Leroux, Paris, 1923.

Labouret Henri, *Les tribus du rameau Lobi*, Institut d'Ethnologie, Paris, 1931.

Ortoli H., *Le gage des personnes au Soudan français*, Bulletin de l'IFAN, Dakar, 1939.

Mercier Paul, *Tradition, changement, histoire, les Somba*, Editions Anthropos, Paris, 1968.

We would like to thank all the inhabitants of the Dogon villages we have visited for their hospitality, helpfulness and understanding for our work. They made it possible for us to share and learn in depth about the public and secret lives of their communities.

Our special thanks go to Ogobara Dolo who, despite his many official duties, found the time to escort us as guide and interpreter, sharing with us his experience, his knowledge and his enthusiasm.

We are particularly gratefull to the following Dogon villagers:

Sanga
Ana Dolo, Urema Dolo, Akorom Dolo, Kembassa Dolo, Dagui Girou, Ambara.

Ireli
Acugnon Baram, his wife Jattegué and his children, Dogoulou and Domo, Ama Guime Dounjon, Ketté Dounjon.

Sedourou
Ibrahim Dara

Nabene
Karoua Dounjon

Kadiavere
Brihm Laya, Akounion Ongenba

Anakila
Omar Aliou

Sirimou
Tetié Cantao, Amadou Komou, Bugapari Komou

Bamba
Guindo Atinbé, Akoundia Guindo

Domnosogou
Ambara Kodio, Adjuro

Ouroukou
Dounj Poundjougo

Pourali
Secu- De

Beniema-na
Amborgo Togo

Diankabou
Boubakar Guindo

Banani
Abinem Girou, Dimogo Girou, Abo Girou, Assegedem Girou, Sagou Birencadiou, Kenné Birencadiou

Daga
Aninou Amono

Amani
Moje Dougon, Atem Aninou, Sirou Ato

Tireli
Gimogo Amono Sai

Mori
Amaiguère Ogobara Dolo, Bandiouma Ombo Timbé, Kanda Ombo Timbé, Pemo Ombo Timbé

Kenndié
Binné Sengepili

Nangadourou
Amaguno Kodio, Adiourou Kodio

Yougodougourou
Agoudjou Doumbo, Menedigem Doumbo, Kennié Doumbo, Ato Doumbo, Amaga Doumbo, Sirou Doumbo

Youngo Na
Kennero Doumbo, Amatigué Doumbo

Yougoplri
Niaba Doumbo, Barhama Doumbo

Neni
Moussa Sagara

Niongono
Sagou Karambé, Bakary Karambé

Barapireli
The White Fathers at the Mission: Du Chouchet, Huguet, Kaiser, Forestier, Anthonissen.

For official permissions and assistance which were vital in carrying out our research:
The Mali Tourist Office
The Mali Security Office
The Mali Immigration Office

INDEX OF NAMES

(The names in italics are in the Dogon language)